The Raj, The Rolls, and The Remorse

PATRICIA YOUNG

The Raj, The Rolls, and The Remorse

A Blighted Life, How Chance Turned It Around,
Yet Remorse Haunted Her All Her Life

authorHOUSE

AuthorHouse™ UK
1663 Liberty Drive
Bloomington, IN 47403 USA
www.authorhouse.co.uk
Phone: 0800.197.4150

© 2018 Patricia Young. All rights reserved.

No part of this book may be reproduced, stored in a retrieval system, or transmitted by any means without the written permission of the author.

This is a work of fiction. All of the characters, names, incidents, organizations, and dialogue in this novel are either the products of the author's imagination or are used fictitiously.

Published by AuthorHouse 10/23/2018

ISBN: 978-1-5462-9787-1 (sc)
ISBN: 978-1-5462-9786-4 (hc)
ISBN: 978-1-5462-9938-7 (e)

Print information available on the last page.

Any people depicted in stock imagery provided by Getty Images are models, and such images are being used for illustrative purposes only. Certain stock imagery © Getty Images.

This book is printed on acid-free paper.

Because of the dynamic nature of the Internet, any web addresses or links contained in this book may have changed since publication and may no longer be valid. The views expressed in this work are solely those of the author and do not necessarily reflect the views of the publisher, and the publisher hereby disclaims any responsibility for them.

Contents

Dedication vi
Introduction vii

Chapter 1   Darjeeling in the 1920s: An Ill-Fated Affair 1
Chapter 2   The Horton Family 8
Chapter 3   Fear of the Family's Wrath 13
Chapter 4   A Possible Solution? 17
Chapter 5   From Darjeeling to Bombay 24
Chapter 6   Secrecy, and Dr Crofton 32
Chapter 7   Birth of Baby Grace, and Heartache 38
Chapter 8   Meeting Edwyn 44
Chapter 9   The SS Ragnera, and Ben 51
Chapter 10 The Rolls Royce 58
Chapter 11 Finding a Home, and Meeting the Brethren 64
Chapter 12 Ten Years Married, and Pregnancy 72
Chapter 13 Leamington Spa, and the War 78
Chapter 14 Back to Domesticity 82
Chapter 15 Dorothy, A Second Marriage, and a New Rolls Royce 86
Chapter 16 Greenacres and Great St Joans 93
Chapter 17 Paris and Other Foreign Parts 104
Chapter 18 Life with Ben 110
Chapter 19 Renewed Faith, and Patricia's Wedding 116
Chapter 20 Ben Dies, and a New Beginning 122
Chapter 21 A Grandchild, and Losing Money 128
Chapter 22 Health Deterioration 134
Chapter 23 Confession 141
Chapter 24 The Closing Stages 147

About the Author 151

Dedication

To my mother.

    How I wish I could have known earlier what you went through in your twenties, as I would now give anything to have you back with me again.

Introduction

My mother had an extraordinary life. Born in 1902, she was brought up with seven brothers in a third-generation British family in India. Aged twenty-four, she had an ill-fated liaison, which left her helpless and nearly ruined her life. However, after meeting her husband-to-be, she took the voyage alone to Britain to start afresh, but a chance meeting on the ship was to change her life.

Writing my mother's story has brought home to me how attitudes to young women becoming pregnant without a supporting partner or husband have radically changed since the 1920s. In India, where my mother grew up, this was the time of the Raj when the British ruled the country and were looked up to by their Indian servants. These servants were employed by the local British to perform all menial tasks, often being paid very little.

Due to the huge difference in social rank, the British were recognised as setting very high standards of behaviour and it was unthinkable that a British girl could become pregnant outside marriage. But my mother did, and the fact that she could not confide in her parents illustrates the shame of how this would have been regarded at the time. British girls were expected to marry first and then have children.

Today, attitudes are different, and some young women often decide to have a child without a partner or husband, and society does not condemn them.

However, my mother lived in a different era, and when she found herself in this position nearly one hundred years ago she would have gone through agonies in her predicament. This is the account of how she tried to forge a new life and put out of her mind what had happened in the past … but she was unable to.

Chapter 1

Darjeeling in the 1920s: An Ill-Fated Affair

The autumn day had been oppressively hot and humid, but now the mist that had temporarily clouded the city of Darjeeling was lifting. By late afternoon, it was a little cooler, although the roads were still dusty, with small areas of caked mud. As usual, there were numerous Indians crowding the streets, as well as the occasional British person. It was 1926. This was the era of the British Raj when white people ruled India. None of them took any particular notice of the young woman walking along the road. She was heading towards the area where many of the British residents lived. Her long, jet-black hair, normally worn in tight braids around her head, hung limply on either side of her face, and she was so absorbed in her thoughts that she was oblivious of the buildings around her. No one was aware that she was apprehensive, confused and *very* frightened.

She came to the area where the majority of the British had their homes. The roads were lined with well-spaced-out, pleasant houses or bungalows, most of which had generous gardens, many containing the huts where the servants lived. Many of the British people who had moved to India in the eighteenth and nineteenth centuries had gone there with the goal of having a better standard of living. Their hopes were fulfilled since, even on mediocre salaries, they were able to employ Indian servants to carry out all the household tasks. The meagre wages they paid in turn made little difference to their savings, thereby allowing them plenty of time and money for active social lives. Ultimately, the British came to control much of the lives of the Indian people.

The young woman, Margaret, slowed her walking pace as she approached her home; she was putting off facing the inevitable meeting with her family. Who could she possibly tell about the situation she found herself in? Not her father or mother and not even any of her seven brothers. In fact, she felt there was no one she could turn to. When she reached the garden gate of their flat-roofed, spacious bungalow, she hesitated. And then she pushed it open and stepped onto the long path that led to the back door.

Her family were third-generation British people, their ancestors having arrived in India in the 1860s. Despite having lived in India all their lives, they sometimes called themselves Anglo-Indians, even though this term was only appropriate when white people married Indians. Their home in the suburbs of Darjeeling was the only life Margaret had known. Although she had been born in Calcutta in 1902, in 1907 her father was posted to Darjeeling and she remembered little of her younger days. She and her family lived as traditional Catholics, as did many of the other British living around them.

As Margaret continued up the garden, several beggars approached. 'Missy, gimme baksheesh,' they said.

Like all the British, she had learned to ignore them and, wrapped up in her own gloomy thoughts, she automatically pushed them away, saying, 'Off with you.'

She was thinking of her parents and how they had always maintained high standards of conduct, especially her mother, who could be quite sharp and severe when any of her children strayed from what she considered acceptable behaviour.

Her father, George Horton, had always worked for the Indian Railways, and now he was the stationmaster at Darjeeling. When he was appointed to this post, the family was thankful to have been transferred from Calcutta to a more pleasant city – this was a hill station with a less exhausting climate. Darjeeling, once a cluster of villages, was now a town that had grown in popularity since the establishment of a major sanatorium in 1839, the cooler climate enticing many of the resident British to spend their holidays there. It became the summer headquarters of the Bengal government and was soon named 'Queen of the Hills'. Imposing Victorian buildings lined the main streets, and the centre of the city was a sought-after and attractive area; many businesses were developing, and the shops now sold increasingly expensive artefacts. Indian sweetmeats and spices abounded, and beggars jostled amongst the rickshaws to make their way through the crowds. Kanchenjunga, the third-highest mountain in the world, towered above the city and was a source of pride to the Indians.

For nearly twenty years, since moving from Calcutta, Margaret had lived here in comparative comfort, although surrounded by abject poverty, dust and creepy crawlies. Indian birds and animals wandered about – even the odd elephant would appear – monkeys played in the trees, and jackdaws would steal your rings. But like the other British people here, her family had a secure and largely stress-free life, mainly due to their ability to employ Indian servants for all their domestic needs. Being surrounded by Hindus and Muslims was perfectly natural to the British since, after Christianity, their faiths had the second and third largest number of believers in the world. The two faiths generally lived peacefully side by side in India, the Hindus believing in reincarnation and karma while the Muslims prayed five times a day and followed the teachings of their prophet Muhammad and their God, Allah. In contrast to this, many of the British adopted the Catholic faith and adhered to it strongly.

Margaret was thinking deeply about her life and how it might have been different in England, but this was the only life she had known and now she found herself in a pitiful situation. Like all the other British people living in Darjeeling, in many ways she had a most enjoyable time. As a white woman, she had little to do other than amuse herself by taking part in the many social activities available, but she now felt that perhaps this was what had caused her present circumstances. Since becoming an adult, she had been to numerous picnics, played a variety of sports – including table tennis, at which she excelled – and been to many dances and balls, chaperoned always, of course, by older ladies. These social occasions formed the normal way of life for the British girls, as it was not considered suitable for them to work. Margaret, now twenty-four, had been out with several young men who were attracted to the warm-hearted, vivacious girl but, so far, she had not returned their affections.

As she continued walking along the garden path, she noticed how the late-afternoon sun had fallen across the veranda. On one side of their fence lived their neighbour, an elderly widower, who had been there ever since Margaret's family had moved to Darjeeling. He had watched her grow up into a delightful young woman and every time he saw her, they would have a little chat; in fact, they were good friends. Now, while watering his roses, he could see her walking slowly up the garden. They always waved when they saw each other, so he waved and called out: 'Hello, Margaret, my dear!'

But this time, she did not appear to hear or notice him, she did not wave back and he wondered why. He waved again and called out, 'Margaret, how was the city today?'

But Margaret gave no response and he immediately sensed that something was wrong. It was so unlike her to ignore him. He had no children of his own and, after his wife had died, he was like an uncle to Margaret. But this afternoon, she appeared distracted and very ill at ease, which was not at all like her usual self. He watched her progress as she passed the rudimentary huts where three of their servants lived, and then disappeared behind some shrubs. He wondered what had made this lovely girl look so troubled and distressed and so he walked a few paces down his garden so that he could see where she had got to.

Margaret had lowered her head and was wandering aimlessly around the thirsty plants and bushes. Her drooping shoulders told him that something had happened recently to make her unhappy. Why, only a few days before, he had seen her in the garden talking animatedly to one of her brothers – laughing, joking, and generally enjoying herself. He was undecided as to whether to walk over to the fence and call out to her again, but after another glance, he felt it was wiser not to. What was it that was causing Margaret such distress? This was what he wanted to know. As it turned out, he was never to know.

Margaret continued to pace around and around the plants and shrubs. In her mind she was reliving the traumatic day, the day that had changed her life. She had spent it in the India Trade and Export Company office in the centre of Darjeeling, a successful company which shipped Indian artefacts all over the world. The company was run by British people, and most of the office staff were British, while the packing staff were Indians.

As the daughter of a British family living in Darjeeling in the 1920s, Margaret would never have gone out to work, but circumstances had changed that. Raina, a very talented Indian lady, the head of sales and director in charge of the company's entertainment, had taken sick leave for four months while recovering from a serious gall bladder operation and the company desperately needed someone to act as social hostess to entertain their clients and suppliers in her absence. One of Margaret's older brothers, Donald, worked for this reputable company, and his boss had persuaded him to ask Margaret if she would come in very occasionally to act in that role. Donald had told him: 'I know she often gets a bit bored at home, but I am sure Mother will not approve. She is pretty strict and very set in her opinion of the way women should conduct themselves. However, I'll ask Margaret, as I feel sure she would be interested.'

His boss fully understood but was pleased that Donald would speak to Margaret. 'It will be hard for us to employ another Indian woman to take the place of Raina,' he explained. 'She has been with us for some years and is as conversant with the suppliers as we are. We cannot engage another person to take Raina's place, as it is only for four months. There are no duties other than engaging clients in conversation, showing them around and keeping them amused. Thank you for saying you'll ask your sister; I'm sure she could get around your mother.'

Donald was very doubtful. When he broached the subject with Margaret, he found she was delighted to be asked, as there were many times at home when she found life rather mundane. Since she was their only daughter, her parents were unusually protective of her. Apart from her brother Albert, who was still at school, her father and other brothers were either out at work or now away from home, and her mother's time was taken up with organising the servants, planning the meals and socialising. Margaret thought it might be rather fun to be out in the city. And, of course, it was only on certain afternoons and for just a few months. However, her mother had refused point blank.

'I am not having you out working, Margaret; white women here never, ever go out to work.' Margaret had tried to get around her by saying: 'Of course not, but this would not be a real job; it's only for four months and on infrequent afternoons, and I would need to wear my best clothes.'

Her mother, Martha Carol, was still very much against it, but with more pleading from Margaret, who intimated that the company were looking for a well-to-do lady, she decided to let her have her way. So, Margaret had started at the company and went in on two afternoons a week. She had a natural gift for making people happy and she took to her role easily and enjoyed it; her warm, friendly nature drew customers to her, and in time the company even found the sales were increasing. They asked her if she could come in more frequently and she did, but on those occasions, knowing that her mother would not allow this, Margaret told her that she was either meeting her friends for afternoon tea or going into the city to shop.

When she had told her friend Kathleen that she wasn't being entirely honest with her mother, Kathleen was taken aback.

'Honestly, Margaret, supposing someone from the company mentioned it to your mother and it all came out?'

'I don't think it will,' said Margaret. 'Since I already go there two afternoons a week, sometimes on different afternoons, it is unlikely that any personnel noticing me will realise I am there more often than usual.'

'Oh goodness, I hope so. I have to say, I envy you having something else to do apart from the usual sports activities and formal meals we have.'

Margaret replied: 'You've only one brother, Kathleen, I have seven: they all adore me and treat me like a princess, but they go off on their own to play team games or polo and I am left at home. When they come back they talk non-stop of all their activities, none of which include me.'

'Well, yes,' said Kathleen, 'I can see how it is, Margaret, and there's no reason why you shouldn't have a bit of life of your own.'

Margaret had agreed and the two giggled a bit and carried on with their girlish chatter.

Leaving the plants and shrubs, Margaret reached the rest of the rambling garden and came to the narrow path which took her to her favourite bench. Here she could be alone without being overlooked by any of the neighbours or even the gardener, and it was out of sight of the two wooden huts where their servants lived. She often came here and would happily sit quietly as the afternoon turned into early evening, but this October afternoon was different. Her lovely face was drained of colour, and her stomach churned uneasily, for she had eaten very little that day.

The smooth skin on her cheeks was taut, her throat felt painful and she wondered if she had an infection, as she felt quite unlike herself. Sheltered family life had not prepared Margaret for her recent circumstances, and a feeling of loneliness swept over her as she thought there was not a living soul who would be able to either understand or help her in this present situation.

On many occasions she had wished she had a sister. She felt this now as never before. She had not been especially emotionally close to any of her older brothers and she searched around in her mind for someone she could talk to. Why could she not talk to her mother? She instinctively knew she could not, would not and should not. Her mother would be utterly scandalised and furious with her, and it was doubtful if she would even try to help. She then thought of her father, sitting benevolently in his chair in the evenings, smoking his pipe, and she knew that even though he adored her and placed her on a pedestal she could not confide in him. Yet she felt desperate to unburden herself to someone. Her good friend Kathleen was the person closest to her and they shared many confidences but, despite this, she hesitated to tell her in case Kathleen was horrified and repeated the news to someone else – there was a strait-laced side to Kathleen and she might be disapproving. But she couldn't delay going in any longer.

Chapter 2

The Horton Family

Slowly getting up from the garden bench, Margaret made her way back to the verandah and into the house. Walking into the sitting room, she looked around at the cheerful rugs on the stone floors and the unfussy rattan furniture in the room. Was this really the same room she had left this morning? It did not seem so, as everything looked so strange.

'I can't face talking to anyone, so I'll go up to my bedroom before anyone sees me,' she thought.

But at that moment her mother walked in and asked if she had enjoyed her time having tea with her friends. Caught on the spur of the moment Margaret was forced to invent a few simple details about her day.

'Oh yes, thank you; we laughed a lot and had a lovely afternoon tea, with scones and honey and delicious fairy cakes,' she said.

Fortunately, Martha Carol was not at all suspicious and simply said that dinner would be at the normal time of 7.00 pm. So, Margaret went up to her bedroom. As usual one of the houseboys had dusted all the furniture there – he did this daily throughout the house, as the dust settled everywhere, and he swept all the floors, ensuring that everything remained neat and tidy. Indoors, the house was kept cool by punkah wallahs, servants who operated a pulley system to sweep heavy curtains backwards and forwards to keep the air moving. Margaret saw that her bedroom was just as she had left it, yet she saw the room with a changed perception, her uneasiness made it appear hostile to her.

'My life is never going to be the same again,' she thought.

As it was not long before the evening meal, she changed her clothes and put her hair into neat braids. When the boy rang the gong to let the family know the meal was ready, Margaret came downstairs, thankful to find that Donald was home, as were her younger brothers Henry and Albert, since this would help deflect her parents' attention away from her.

She took her place at the dinner table and contemplated her family. Her father, George Horton, was a solid, gentle, reliable man whose job title was Traffic Inspector for Darjeeling Station, but he was otherwise known as the Stationmaster. The station had survived an earthquake in 1892 and a cyclone in 1899, but by the time the Hortons arrived in 1907 the station had recovered and was up and running well. George's job was considered a very responsible one, as the arrival and departure times of trains at this time were so unpredictable. They were seldom punctual, often an hour or more late arriving or leaving, and sometimes they had been known to be a day late and so he was constantly phoned by people wanting the latest train information. The Horton family were well known in the city and enjoyed an active social life with the other British people there.

The Darjeeling Himalayan Railway had been built between 1879 and 1881, and it provided links to the towns and cities further south. At the beginning of the twentieth century, the British had played an important part in the development and running of the railway system in India and the Railway Institute, an imposing, gracious building near the station, with impressively decorated rooms, was a focal point for them. The railway employees and their families enjoyed the many social activities held there, as well as making friendships and, of course, gossip… Well-dressed English ladies met there for lunch and afternoon tea – their meals were served on expensive china with dainty napkins. When they could get hold of magazines or books of European fashions, these were studied carefully and local dressmakers were ordered to copy the designs. Dinners were frequently held and were occasions on which the women could wear these fine dresses.

The Institute had sports grounds for tennis, squash, cricket and table tennis – a particular favourite, and hockey and badminton were also popular. Because of the heat, these were normally played towards the end of the day. The children played rounders, hopscotch and marbles – the warm climate meant that children could play mainly out of doors. Board games were popular too as were skittles, bridge and amateur theatre. Family picnics on the Institute's lawns were frequent except in the monsoon months when the rain poured down incessantly. The British had no problem in finding some form of social amusement. Margaret was often there since she loved playing table tennis whenever she could find a partner to play with. In fact, she had become so good that she had won the Railway Institute ladies' table tennis tournament for four consecutive years.

Indeed, the British enjoyed a far better lifestyle than they would have had in England since having Indian servants to take over all the domestic duties freed them for more social activities. Their children were cared for meticulously by an ayah, a woman similar to a nanny or nursemaid. Margaret and her seven brothers had all been looked after in this way and, as the only girl, Margaret had understandingly become their Ayah's favourite. But now no ayahs were needed, as all eight children were grown up. Martha Carol was kept busy overseeing the servants: the cook, the boy who served at table, another boy who cleaned the house and ran errands, plus the gardener; not forgetting the dhobi who came weekly to collect the washing and bring back the ironed clothes. And, finally, the emptying of the commodes was done by the lowest caste of Indians, known as the Untouchables.

Although these servants earned a pittance, they were in a better position than the thousands of Indians who had no work at all. Those poor mortals lived pitiful lives in the scattered outlying villages with barely a roof over their heads, some of them with not even enough food or water. For the British living in India it soon became normal to be surrounded by Indians existing in poverty. During the days of the Raj when Britain ruled India, the Indians knew their place was to be subservient to the British – their livelihood depended on it.

By comparison with a woman in England with eight children in the 1920s, Margaret's mother enjoyed a far better life. She had all the servants she needed and she just had to give orders to each one and the task was done. All the rooms in the large bungalow were kept clean and tidy and, despite the heat, the garden was cared for. The furniture in the British homes was generally made of relatively light materials such as bamboo, cane or wicker, as this helped to keep the house cool. The floors were stone with rugs thrown over them. Family meals were taken in style, with nicely laid tables, linen napkins and good-quality china. The servants prepared all the meals, and after they had served the first course, they would wait quietly until the family were ready for the next course and then bring it in. The British tended to eat a mixture of home food and Indian and so Cook would be taught how to cook British food as well as producing meals based on the Indian cuisine. Although the Indians never took to British food, the British in general came to enjoy the spicier Indian meals.

The Horton family was not rich, but George Horton's position as the Traffic Inspector gave them a certain standing in the city. They were well-known, revered and respected by the other British, and of course, by the local Indians. However, despite George's comfortable and well-regarded position, he occasionally wished for even greater status for himself and his family and wondered if they would have had more standing if he had gone into the army. The British Army in Darjeeling was of considerable importance in the city and the surrounding area. As the British controlled and ruled their country at this time, the Indians living there were in considerable awe of the British Army and looked up to them with the greatest respect.

Yet all his sons were doing well, and his happy and beautiful daughter, Margaret, was adored by every one of her brothers and respected by everyone else around her. George had always hoped she would make a good marriage, but here she was at twenty-four and still there was no hint of a serious romance in her life.

'She's taking her time about it,' he said to his wife. 'She has had plenty of chances but somehow she seems to veer away from any man who becomes serious. I want her to get married soon and settle down and have a family, so we can have more grandchildren.'

Martha Carol agreed. 'I don't know what it is with her,' she replied. 'I sometimes feel she seems a little restless, and recently she has been going out more and more. It is all tea parties, picnics, dances and balls, none of which seem to lead anywhere.'

'I had hoped we would have more girls,' George maintained, 'but we did not, and I'm sure that being the only girl with so many brothers has at times seemed a trifle strange to Margaret.'

'I agree,' responded his wife. 'Maybe I have not given her the attention she needs. I have tried to give her a practical upbringing, but somehow she's in a world of her own; besides, she is so different from me, I find it almost impossible to reach her.'

George Horton said no more and neither did Martha Carol, but they both had uneasy thoughts going around in their minds.

Chapter 3

Fear of the Family's Wrath

George Horton continued to reflect on whether he would have been better off in the army, as it seemed to him that army life held more superior social events and he felt that his family were often excluded from those in Darjeeling. But in thinking this, he was largely mistaken – it was only the very small and select parties held on grand regal occasions to which they were not invited. However, he remembered when the daughter of the chief administrator of the British Army in West Bengal was married and they were not invited – this still rankled with him.

George was determined, and so was Martha Carol, that Margaret, with her beauty, charm and natural gaiety, should marry one of the top-ranking British Army officers. If not, they hoped she would find a wealthy man at the Railway Institute, where many of the social activities took place. Picnics, dances, games and even the occasional ball were customary. Of course, there were other events in Darjeeling to which they were invited, but the Railway Institute was their main source of entertainment. Afternoon tea was always an occasion and it would be served there with the best-quality china and small, delicious cakes.

Margaret was deep in thought about everything that had made up her life so far, and how secure and trouble-free it had been, but how it had now suddenly all changed. 'How can I have come to this?' she thought. 'My life has been so stable and none of us have ever disgraced our family, yet now I am about to do this. Father and Mother will both be utterly horrified;

as for my brothers, who idolise me, they will find it hard to believe what has happened.'

Margaret had been born the fourth child of eight. As well as Donald, she had two other older brothers, Howard and Leonard, and four younger ones, Henry, Bernard, Albert and William. Thinking of them now, she realised her brothers were almost a clan. Whatever one of them wanted to do there was always another brother who would join in. It was not that the brothers had excluded her, as in some ways they treated her like a queen. But Margaret had times when she felt isolated from them all; she had never been very close to any of the older ones and had spent more time with the four younger ones. When the Indian servants would let her, she had often played at mothering the four younger boys and was very fond of them all. The older boys had always had each other and had considered her too 'girlish' to include in whatever they were doing. Margaret had tried on several occasions to get involved in some of the sports in which her brothers took part, but it was not normal in the 1920s for girls to be included in strenuous sports since this was not considered ladylike, and so this was one more thing that she had been left out of.

Now, Howard, her eldest brother by ten years, lived in Bombay and was busy developing his wine and spirit export business. Leonard, a fervent and devoted Catholic, was also living away, in Nagpur, working for a British firm manufacturing iron and steel. Although Howard and Leonard came home every few months, there never seemed time for Margaret to get to know either of them in a deeper way. She did see more of Donald, since he worked for the India Trade and Export Company, where she had her part-time job. And at twenty-four, despite an active, social lifestyle, she had in fact led a comparatively sheltered life and was still a little in awe of her older brothers.

Her youngest brother, Albert, was about to leave school, while William was at college studying engineering. Henry and Bernard had both recently started work; Henry was settling into the army and was billeted here in Darjeeling, and Bernard was training to work for the prison service and expecting to be sent to the Andaman Islands for a couple of years. Margaret knew that Henry, Bernard, William and Albert adored and respected her as their older sister, and all of them would do anything in the world she asked, believing there was not another girl in Darjeeling like her.

But Margaret knew in her heart that since the younger boys all thought she was the perfect sister, they would be unable to understand her present situation. No, none of the younger brothers could help her.

As she looked around the dinner table, she was surprised to find that everything seemed just as normal. It was she who had changed. So confused and tortured was she that she did not notice the boy had laid an extra place and she sat down without realising that her eldest brother, Howard, had joined them. She had completely forgotten he was coming for a week's visit. Normally she would have been pleased to see him, but now she just stared at him and struggled to smile, hardly aware of his presence. As one of the Indian servants handed the food around, Margaret was struggling to eat and avoided everyone's glance, especially her mother's. Martha Carol was not one for talking a lot, but she was a stickler for order and punctuality. She was a rather stern lady who did not show a lot of affection towards her children, but perhaps with seven boys she needed to be somewhat severe to keep them all in order. She acted similarly with Margaret, who, being of an outgoing, warm and expressive nature, had longed to feel close to her mother, but never felt able to be so. Margaret looked at her now and for a fleeting moment she considered confiding in her, but the thought lasted merely seconds and she instantly dismissed it, knowing how unwise that would be.

Howard had arrived that afternoon and already he was wondering why Margaret had not made an effort to welcome him. Usually she was at home during the day, but he knew she was helping out at the India Trade and Export Company in the city, and yet she seemed to have quite forgotten he was coming. She looked somewhat paler than usual, did not seem at all her normal vivacious self and he noticed how agitated she seemed. He wondered what was amiss. As he stared at her, Margaret looked across the table at him, and immediately dropped her eyes, avoiding his questioning gaze. Howard said nothing, but he knew instinctively something was wrong. As the eldest child and ten years older than her, he had always kept an eye on his only sister when he was at home, and now he felt a certain responsibility to discover what was upsetting her so much. He hazarded a guess that it could be something that she felt unable to share with the family.

Once the family meal was finished the servants brought in the Darjeeling tea. After drinking his tea, Howard suggested casually: 'Margaret, would you like to come to the Pattagore Gardens for a drink tonight?'

Both his father and mother looked pleased to see him taking an interest in his sister and since they knew this was a fitting place for Margaret to go, they were happy that she would be chaperoned by her eldest brother. The Gardens were nearby and had a congenial and friendly atmosphere. Her father said: 'That's kind of you, Howard. I know Margaret would like this and she loves to dance.'

And Margaret, now at her wits end, jumped at the chance to talk to her brother alone and so she replied: 'That would be good fun, I love it there. It's such a jolly place and you can have a drink and watch people dancing, and you can dance too.'

'Come on then, we'll go now,' responded Howard.

Margaret fetched her shawl and they went out together. They walked on for a bit, then Howard lit a cigarette but decided not to probe his sister. He was of a quiet, practical nature, but also sensitive to people's feelings. After walking on in silence for a few minutes, Margaret suddenly turned towards him and clutched his arm, saying: 'I have got something awful to tell you, Howard. I am in a dreadful position. I cannot believe what has happened to me. You are going to be absolutely shocked to hear what it is. Before I tell you, you must promise me never to tell another living soul, especially no one in our family.'

Chapter 4

A Possible Solution?

On hearing his sister speak like this, Howard was totally mystified. He could not imagine what had happened in her life to provoke this anguish; surely it must be something relatively trivial, something that with his help could easily be put right. Perhaps one of the other brothers or someone else had upset her badly?

Whatever it was, he would do his best to resolve the problem for her. Knowing Margaret to be easily swayed by her emotions, he felt the problem could easily be remedied.

They were very close to the Gardens now; Margaret was quietly sobbing, so he put his arm around her to give her some support. Once inside, Howard found a small corner table away from the noise and the majority of the people there and got her a small glass of lassi, a mixture of yoghourt and water, to calm her down. Margaret had stopped sobbing, but tears were running down her face and Howard tried in vain to calm her so that she could tell him what was wrong. It took a few minutes until she was able to hesitantly say: 'A week ago I thought… I might be going to have a baby, and when I went to see Dr Brownlow this morning he told me I am two and a half months' pregnant. I have started to feel a bit sick, and the worst thing is I don't think the father will marry me. In fact, I know he definitely won't, as this afternoon when I told him about the baby he did not want to know about it, and then he told me he was married and he intended to stay married. I just can't believe it; I had absolutely no idea and all along I thought we would be getting married.'

Howard was a dependable and trustworthy man, generally rather reserved, but he had a kindly side to his nature. He tried very hard to cover up his dismay, but in spite of himself he could not help letting out a gasp of disbelief. In 1920s' India it was absolutely unheard of for well-to-do British girls to get pregnant outside marriage. Howard gently asked her to let him know more about what had happened.

'How on earth did you not find out sooner that he was married?' he queried. 'Surely someone must have mentioned it? Anyway, who is he and how did you meet him?'

Margaret knew that she would have to tell the whole story.

'As you know, from time to time, I've been acting as social hostess for the Entertainment department of the India Trade and Export Company. Just temporarily, as the director for Entertainment is on sick leave for four months recovering from a serious gall bladder operation. It's only for their most important clients and suppliers and it has only been occasionally, but then a large order came in which needed several weeks' preparation before being shipped to Calcutta. The managers were hard-pressed in overseeing the order and needed to use some of the administrative staff to help them. And so they asked if I could be available to welcome incoming visitors and direct them to the right department.'

'I am sure Mother was not at all happy about this?' enquired Howard.

'No, she was not happy at all, and I had to fib about the extra time; I know it was wrong, but I so enjoyed getting out and having something positive to do; I love my time there.'

'I do understand that, but how did you meet this man, Margaret?'

'I had to work with one of the younger export directors, Gordon McCall. We spent quite a bit of time together, and he fell in love with me, or so I thought, and I fell violently in love with him. He told me how my gift of talking easily to anyone and socialising was a benefit to the company. One afternoon we were alone and he told me he was in love with me; I believed him and I was sure we were going to get married, but now I look back on it, he has never said anything about marriage. It must have been me who imagined it.'

'How could you possibly have been so naïve, Margaret?' said Howard.

'I know, I should have made certain he was not married and I did not. And now I'm a woman without a husband who is expecting a baby.'

Howard was totally stunned; this was not at all what he had expected. Nothing like this had ever happened in their family. Their Catholic faith had given them strong convictions as to right and wrong and their parents had instilled these beliefs into all eight of their children. He gently pressed her to tell him more.

Margaret continued that although her upbringing had not accustomed her to any form of work, she had slipped easily into her role at the export company. Indeed, it was not really a role but allowed her to use her own natural attributes. She was never asked to do any administrative work, and only went into the office when the company needed her. At first, she could not remember the names of the directors she met, but as she came to know them better she found this easier and felt relaxed when she met them. Two or three of the directors found that Margaret's friendly and easy manner with their clients was good for business and some of the clients even started to ask if Margaret would be at certain functions. Although she was far from being a sharp-minded businesswoman, she was conscientious and had started to learn enough about the business to be able to help clients enjoy mixing business with leisure. It was not long before Gordon McCall realised with satisfaction that the company's entertaining profile was becoming a major force in the area. Of course, it was not all due to Margaret, but she had helped him work on a number of the entertaining plans, and somehow she provided a charm and graciousness which the Indian head of sales, now away convalescing, had not.

Once or twice Margaret had spent the whole day at the office, preparing plans for a grand occasion. She knew how important the company's entertaining profile was to Gordon and was happy to work the extra hours. The atmosphere in the India Trade and Export company offices was a surprise to her, as it was not as rigid and structured as she had thought it would be. The British male staff were more than happy for her to use her natural warmth with clients, as it spared them from having to do this themselves. Margaret's help had allowed Gordon to get a couple of the events prepared on time and he had been most appreciative. He was a man with an easy banter who laughed a lot, but he was not a deep thinker and some of the people who knew him well found him to be rather shallow. However, Gordon was a breath of fresh air for Margaret. Left to her own devices at home she had often felt bored and lonely and so she loved being surrounded by people and enjoyed organising things which brought pleasure to them. Gordon came across as kind and understanding, and never pressed her to do more than she could, so she very quickly felt at ease with him. After being at the office for six weeks, Margaret missed it on the days she did not go in. Gordon and Margaret had, in fact, become close working associates; they laughed and joked a lot together and Margaret valued his friendship enormously.

She continued speaking to Howard. 'Then one afternoon in August the other directors had all gone to a luncheon in town, and Gordon and I were together in his office. He came over to me and quietly told me that he loved me. I had never thought of him in a romantic way until then, but his persuasive manner touched me and I found myself responding to him. Compared to the young men I usually meet, he had a slightly more sophisticated air about him.'

'Margaret, you have been duped, my poor girl. You have always been gullible and would swallow any tall story. You were a sitting target for this man,' lamented Howard.

Margaret then told him that later that week, in Gordon's office, they became lovers. It was the first time that she had been intimate with a man, and from the words Gordon spoke to her she'd inferred that in time they would get married. It seemed no one was suspicious of them, and their relationship continued blissfully for another month. Margaret, deeply involved in her first real love affair, told no one about it and felt secure in Gordon's love. Apart from somewhat vague and romantic ideas about the wedding they would have and their future life together, which she mentioned to him from time to time, she gave no thought to anything else. Gordon had suggested they keep their relationship a secret for a while and although Margaret had hazily wondered why they should do this she had no trouble in agreeing.

As she poured out her anguish to Howard, Margaret felt some relief – at least she had found someone to share her agonies with, and he did not appear critical of her. She had never spoken to him like this before – the age gap between them meant that they had never been very close. But Howard had always taken notice of his only sister and respected her.

To hear that she had been having an affair with a married man was an unexpected shock to him. He did not say much but quietly intimated that he fully understood her situation and asked her to tell him anything else she needed to.

'After I'd seen Dr Brownlow, I went straight to Gordon's office to tell him about the baby. I felt sure he would now ask me to marry him. I was anxious to tell our parents and all my brothers. But, as I said, it had never entered my head that he was married, as he had never mentioned a word about his wife.'

Howard could see that it had been shattering news to her, to suddenly know she had been having an affair with a married man and was now expecting his child. It was not difficult for him to fully comprehend why she felt herself to be in such a helpless situation.

Margaret continued: 'Even when he told me he was married, I was still hoping he might get a divorce so that we could be married, but he said…'

Margaret couldn't go on; she remembered how Gordon had given her a rueful smile and, turning his face away from her, had said: 'Margaret, my darling, of course we love each other, but as I said before I am already married, and I've every intention of staying married. I'm sorry you are going to have a baby, but I'll never, ever leave my wife, and you'll have to have an abortion. You can see one of the Indians who'll do this for you and I'll pay for it, so no one need ever know anything about it.'

Margaret turned to Howard. 'When I heard this, I was completely taken aback because since I'd suspected I might be pregnant I'd experienced strong feelings of a bond with the little person inside me. When Gordon talked about having an abortion I was horrified – I'd heard a little about these backstreet Indian abortionists from one of my girlfriends.' Certainly no one in Margaret's family spoke about this sort of thing, and she had a hazy idea that only Indian woman had abortions. As she told Howard, the conversation with Gordon had left her emotions in turmoil for the rest of the day. She had tried to speak to him again, but he had made it clear he was not interested in the baby, and he wanted her to get rid of it.

As all this was revealed to Howard, the evening's entertainment at the Pattagore Gardens went on as usual. People around them were laughing and drinking, couples were dancing, and the music played on. Margaret was so distressed she was unaware of all this. Fortunately, Howard had listened to her story with patience and compassion, aware that his sister was in some ways inexperienced and knew little about the world around her. He realised, too, that he had never really looked on Margaret as an adult or treated her as one. Yet, here she was expecting a baby, and he wondered what on earth he could do to help her. Although he was far less straitlaced than Margaret feared, he found it embarrassing to talk to her about such very personal matters. However, he felt he must discuss it with her, so he said: 'Did you talk to Dr Brownlow about having an abortion with a British doctor?'

'No, I didn't ask him, and he didn't offer it to me. I think he thought I had a serious man friend who would marry me, and I didn't tell him otherwise. In any case, I could not think about an abortion, the idea is too dreadful; the thought of killing my unborn child is unthinkable, and I would never consider it.'

Howard said nothing, and although abortion was not accepted by Catholics he thought in this case she was making the wrong decision. He did, of course, understand why she was feeling this way, so he nodded to show his empathy and put his arm around her in a protective manner.

It was getting late, the music was still playing, glasses littered the tables, some couples were still dancing and the evening at the Pattagore Gardens went on in its usual lively way. In silence, they walked back to the house, Howard's arm still around Margaret. They both knew without saying that no other member of their family would believe she had been having an affair with a married man, let alone that she was now pregnant – so far, she had managed to conceal from her mother that she hadn't needed her monthly towels. After all she belonged to a united, stable and happy Catholic family. But now she had let the family down and, knowing this, Margaret felt a deep sense of remorse and a feeling that she had cut herself off from her family. The quiet, somewhat remote and hardworking father, and the upright, respectable and conscientious mother would both be crushed by the unacceptable news. And her other brothers? It did not bear thinking about, and more panic welled up in Margaret. She turned to Howard: 'Father and Mother must never, ever know.'

Howard totally agreed with her, yet he could not think of any way in which this could be avoided. As they walked home, they passed one of the local bazaars that was still open. Margaret adored the bazaars – she would stay for an hour or more looking at the gaily coloured Indian jewellery, charms and trinkets. She had a way of choosing inexpensive necklaces, bracelets and earrings that suited her colouring and went with her clothes. But today she passed the bazaar without giving it a second glance. It was dark now and they walked on in silence, both absorbed in their own thoughts. Only a few lights lit the road; Margaret was conscious of the gloom and it just made her feel more depressed. They were nearly home when an idea suddenly came to Howard.

'Margaret,' he said. 'In a week I will be going back to my home in Bombay. If you came with me I think I could pass you off as a young widow, and maybe even find you something to occupy yourself with until the baby is born. I know a British family there with two young children and they are looking for an English girl to look after them. You have always been good at caring for your younger brothers, so you might be able to fill your time by being a Nanny to them. You could live with me until the baby is born and I am sure it would not be difficult for people to accept that you were a widow.'

Margaret did not reply for a couple of minutes, as the thought of moving to a huge city like Bombay and leaving all her family in Darjeeling, where she had spent the greater part of her life, terrified her. Howard continued: 'There's enough room in my apartment for you, and my boy can cope with looking after us both. We need not ever tell Father or Mother, or any of our brothers – not one of them need ever know. And if you are able to do some childminding work for this family, you'll have a chance to save up a bit of money, so that you can have the baby in one of the best British hospitals in Bombay.'

Margaret was utterly bewildered and was having difficulty taking in Howard's suggestion. She felt fearful at the idea of leaving her family, her friends and all the familiar things in Darjeeling which were dear to her. But she could also understand that Howard's idea was a wonderful opportunity, and a solution to all her problems, provided of course that their parents were happy about it. She lowered her voice, and whispered to him: 'It's a brilliant idea, Howard, but … dare we do it?'

Chapter 5

From Darjeeling to Bombay

By the time they arrived home, they were both convinced of the wisdom of Margaret leaving with Howard when he returned to Bombay the following week. Margaret was feeling extremely nervous and hoped her parents had gone to bed. But they found their parents sitting quietly in the lounge, where they had been waiting up to be sure Margaret was safely back. Howard and Margaret both sat down, Howard choosing a chair where he could look directly at both his father and mother. He casually explained his plan to them, taking care to show how beneficial it would be for his sister to come and stay with him for a few months, as it would expand her social life and give her a chance to meet new people. He hinted that he would be able to introduce her to some suitable men. Both parents were a bit surprised to hear this but also delighted that Howard would go out of his way to give his sister this opportunity. When they realised it would be for only a few months they could see the advantages for her and they soon had no trouble in agreeing to it – in fact, they were very happy that Margaret would be able to live in such a big city and have the opportunity to meet more suitable men there than she had so far in Darjeeling.

George Horton, generally somewhat aloof and a bit distant, puffed away on his pipe and said he was so pleased that Margaret would be able to meet new people and she would always have her eldest brother, Howard, to protect her. Martha Carol, although outwardly rather stern and strict, was also very protective of Margaret, but she soon came around to the proposal.

It was time her daughter thought about getting married, and she was aware that with seven brothers Margaret was often left to make her own life, as the brothers banded together for their activities. She warmly expressed her approval to Howard and came over to give her daughter a hug. Knowing she was deceiving her parents, Margaret immediately felt uneasy, but she also felt immense relief to find them fully in agreement with Howard's proposal. She tried not to show how fearful she would be to have to cope without her familiar surroundings and without all those who were dear to her. A feeling of remorse swept over her again and for a moment she nearly revealed her pregnancy; however, the fact that none of her family or anyone else in Darjeeling need ever know about the baby was enough for her to bury the impulse and seize the opportunity her brother was offering her.

The next week passed in preparations for Margaret's departure. The servants were instructed to pack her trunk with most of her possessions and clothes. Her mother told her to buy herself two new dresses, which Margaret did, smiling a bit forlornly as she knew she would be unable to wear them for quite some time. The whole house was geared to her departure and everyone seemed to be in a turmoil of excitement. The servants busied about fetching this and that and making sure Margaret's clothes were immaculate. Friends were invited over to talk about the opportunity Margaret was to have to stay with her brother in Bombay, and how she would return home in a few months' time. Howard talked cheerfully about parties, dances and balls, and the contacts he had through both his business and social life.

'I have a lively social life in Bombay,' he said. 'I've been living there for nearly ten years and I know a lot of people now. There are a great many British people there, including many single men who either live there permanently or are on secondment from British industries. In fact, there are never enough women since the men far outnumber them. So, Margaret will have a good time, she will meet new people and I know she will be popular.'

Listening to Howard talk about the number of single men in Bombay, George and Martha Carol were even more satisfied that Howard was offering Margaret this opportunity, and the four younger brothers came to think how lucky she was. No one was the least suspicious and even Margaret's girlfriends thought how fortunate she was. The worst part was not being able to tell her close friend Kathleen the truth – this pained Margaret a lot. Two days before she left, they met to say goodbye. Kathleen said how much she would miss her, which moved Margaret nearly to tears. Kathleen had been Margaret's special friend since they were teenagers, they saw a lot of each other and often went to picnics and tea dances together. Kathleen knew that Margaret had been working extra days at the India Trade and Export Company, as she had told her, but she did not know the whole story. Margaret's stomach was turning over when she saw Kathleen and it took all her resolve to act naturally with her special friend, especially when she did not know when she would see her again. She longed to tell her the truth but knew she must not. Worse still, she knew Kathleen would have understood, but she still thought it better to keep silent.

Margaret went into the India Trade and Export Company and explained her brother's plans. She told them that she had always wanted to visit Bombay and now this was a chance not to be missed. Providentially, Raina, the Indian director, was shortly coming back from sick leave. Margaret dreaded facing Gordon McCall again, as her heart was still aching from their previous encounter, but the day before she left, she went in to say goodbye to him. He gave her a gentle hug and handed her a bundle of notes, saying she would need these for her abortion. Margaret did not want to tell him she intended to keep the baby, so she thanked him and took the money. Afterwards she expressed to Howard how appalling she had felt when she saw Gordon again.

'I'm still in love with him. Of course, I know he has deceived me and behaved very badly to me, but I loved him a lot and I find I still do. Seeing him again brought it all back to me.'

And Howard, knowing how heartbroken Margaret was, realised what a traumatic time his sister was going through, and he wanted to get her away as soon as possible. 'I know, it must be pretty harrowing for you. But we'll manage; I'll look after you and once we get to Bombay you'll feel different.'

And Margaret replied: 'All I can feel now is regret at the mistake I've made and the situation I'm in.'

Howard could not find words to hearten her. The following day it was time to leave for Darjeeling station. Margaret wished desperately that she could tell her family the truth, and she only just managed not to. The worst thing was saying goodbye to her parents, her younger brothers, and even the servants, who had been part of her life for so many years; indeed, some of them cried when she said goodbye to them. Her large family had surrounded her with love, care and protection, and now suddenly she was to be thrust into the huge city of Bombay, a city she knew nearly nothing about. Above all, she was anxious as to how Howard would manage to keep her secret and pass her off as a young widow.

Margaret's mother, rarely a demonstrative lady, gave her a kiss and said how much she would miss her, but fortunately it was only for a few months. Margaret nearly broke down and once again almost told her mother the truth but managed to smile at everyone and put on a cheerful front. Her father hugged her, then gave her some money and said he was looking forward to her return. Howard and Margaret left for the station. The minute the train started Margaret had the sensation that she was cut off from all her familiar and safe life, and feelings of grief and guilt washed over her.

India was such a vast country that travelling from Darjeeling to Bombay in the 1920s necessitated changing trains twice, and it took nearly three days to get there. True to form, the trains rarely arrived or left on time and as Margaret had never travelled so far before, she found the waiting around on stations totally exhausting. She was still feeling sick in the mornings and being constantly surrounded by the chatter of people took its toll. She would look around at the other people on the trains and stations and imagine they all led happy and peaceful lives, unmarred by misfortune or calamity. On one occasion this must have shown in her expression, as an older Indian lady in her carriage spoke to her: 'Why are you looking so forlorn and unhappy, my darling?'

And Margaret, shaken into thinking that everyone could read her problems on her face, attempted to speak cheerfully, and replied: 'I am going to stay with my brother in Bombay for a while and I am finding the journey tiresome. I have not travelled so far before and I am missing my family in Darjeeling.'

The Indian lady, interested in why Margaret was travelling to Bombay, went on to ask about her family and her life in Darjeeling, but fortuitously Margaret remembered what Howard had said about not revealing any details about herself and said: 'Train journeys always make me feel a bit unwell, so I am going to have a sleep now.'

Fortunately for Margaret, the older lady left her alone and did not worry her again.

Before they had set off, Howard had realised that the journey would tire Margaret, and he did his best to talk cheerfully and to protect her from any inconveniences that could arise.

'Every hour takes us nearer to Bombay,' he said. 'Sit down on this seat and try to make yourself comfortable. At the next stop I'll get out and get us something to eat.'

'I'm trying to,' Margaret replied, 'but I keep being pushed about by those around me.'

'That's hard, I know,' said Howard, and he moved so she could lean against him.

After three days the wearisome journey ended, and they arrived at Bombay station as night fell. Once on the crowded platform, they made their way outside and Howard found a space for their luggage on the pavement. He told Margaret: 'Sit on your trunk, don't talk to anyone and mind you keep an eye on my case. I'm going to get a rickshaw.'

A rickshaw duly arrived with Howard in it, the luggage was piled in and they set off for Howard's apartment. The rickshaw ride was bumpy and as they travelled along the crowded roads Margaret felt overwhelmed by the seething mass of natives, which the rickshaw driver was relentlessly fighting his way through. Howard took great pains to see that Margaret was as comfortable as possible, and after about half an hour they finally arrived at his apartment. Margaret had, of course, never been in his home but utterly worn out both physically and emotionally she was thankful to fall into bed. Howard's houseboy was there and seeing how exhausted she was, he brought her some tea, saying: 'Missy drink tea, Missy feel better.'

It was not her beloved Darjeeling tea, nevertheless it was good, strong Indian tea, and Margaret drank it and fell into a deep sleep for sixteen hours and it was mid-morning before she woke up. Howard's apartment seemed so small compared to her family's roomy bungalow in Darjeeling. He had left her a note to say he had gone off to work and would be back at lunchtime to see that she was all right. The houseboy brought her some breakfast, and as she looked around the apartment she had a sense of isolation: used to being surrounded by her brothers, her parents and the servants, she missed them all. Now there was just the two of them and

Howard's boy, and Howard would be out all day at his office in the centre of Bombay. Margaret decided not to leave the apartment until Howard could show her around the area. He came back at lunchtime and told her to stay in the apartment that day, but the following day, being Sunday, he would take her out.

On Sunday they went out together and Howard showed Margaret around the area and the useful shops she would need. She found the city stiflingly hot and so much more intense than in Darjeeling. Cyclists were everywhere, calling out and shouting to each other as they made their way through the streets, while rickshaws were being dragged and pushed through the crowds, all throwing up dirt and dust. She desperately missed the familiar and customary ways of her home.

When Howard returned to work the following day, Margaret did not dare venture out for more than a few minutes, as she was fearful of not finding her way back. It was now that she had to face the reality of her situation – she was going to have a baby, she had practically no money and how on earth was she going to cope in the future?

Howard let her settle down for a week until the exhaustion passed and Margaret started to feel less sick and more at ease in her surroundings. His apartment was pleasant and in a quieter district of the city than most, and before long she felt herself calming down. He had introduced her to his fiancée, Nora, hoping the two of them would get on. Nora was a down-to-earth lady, very practical, and Margaret found her sensible attitude to matters brought some measure of calm to her life. At the same time, Margaret realised that Nora was keen for her marriage to Howard to take place before too long, and she felt she must be a burden to them both.

Howard warned her to always say to anyone who spoke to her that she was a widow whose husband had died young from a sudden heart attack.

As she became more comfortable with her surroundings, during the day she would wander around the nearby streets, thronged with Indian ladies dressed in their bright, colourful saris, a garment created many hundreds of years before, which they had worn ever since. The original dyes – such as indigo, red madder and turmeric – were still in use. She did not venture far since the seething masses confused her, but on one occasion when she did she saw, lying in the gutter, a dead body and was horrified. Her pregnancy meant she never got used to Bombay's hotter climate, and at odd times she still felt nauseated and depressed. Fortunately, Howard had lost no time in introducing her to the British couple he had spoken to her about. Ben and Rosalind Grant with their two young children lived only a fifteen-minute walk from his apartment. He spoke to them, explaining that Margaret had been widowed recently, and Rosalind Grant asked him if he would please bring her round to meet them, which he did.

'How very sad for you,' Rosalind Grant said to Margaret. She was genuinely sympathetic towards her and also very gratified to find such a well-educated British girl to care for her two precious children, as she suffered from a bad back and needed to rest in the afternoons. Howard did most of the talking and explained about Margaret's younger brothers and how good she was with them. Rosalind Grant was most taken with Margaret and the thought that she would look after Michael, aged four, and Mary, aged two, pleased her enormously. The children were brought in, clutching their toys, and Margaret, immediately at ease with young children, spoke to them.

'Hello Michael, I hear you go to proper school in the mornings now? Have you been today?'

Michael showed her a man he had made with cardboard that morning.

'Yes, today I made this man and I didn't have any help from my teacher.'

'That's very lifelike, Michael, well done,' said Margaret. 'Are you going to colour him?'

'I would like to, but I need to choose which colours to use.'

Margaret looked at the box of colours, and helped him to choose three, which he immediately started using.

She turned to Mary, who was looking expectantly at her. 'Could you show me what's in your box, Mary?'

The little girl brought out a small doll and showed it to Margaret, who said: 'Is that your favourite doll, Mary?'

Mary, who was a bit shy, nodded and gave the doll to Margaret, who admired it and then gave it back to her, saying: 'Perhaps we can have a tea party one day for your doll? Would you like that?'

And Mary, delighted at this idea, smiled at Margaret and said: 'Yes please,' and she took out a small tea set from her box and started to put the parts on the nearby table.

Rosalind Grant quickly saw that Margaret had a gift with young children and engaged her immediately. She was so relieved to have found someone so clearly suitable to look after her children, so it was arranged that Margaret would come over to their home every afternoon for four hours to care for them. The Grants had a delightful, comfortably furnished home with several servants, and as Margaret was used to having Indian servants around she felt totally at ease there. They were prepared to pay well for such a suitable nanny and it was arranged that Margaret would start at once. It was by no means an onerous task and Margaret found she loved her little job and the two children soon took to her. Concentrating on the children's needs took her mind away from her circumstances, and she felt secure with the British family, who totally accepted that she was a widow and seldom made any reference to it. In no time Margaret found going to the Grants made an immense difference to how she felt, and her mood lifted. Earning money helped too, and feeling that she was doing something worthwhile, her confidence increased. Howard noticed the change in her and was greatly relieved. After going to the Grants for a fortnight Margaret remarked to Howard: 'I can't believe how much happier I feel having something to do again. It seems so natural looking after the children. I particularly remember Albert and William when they were young, and how I would beg our Ayah to let me look after them.'

'Yes, I remember that too,' replied Howard, smiling. 'I always thought you were a little mother even when you were young.'

They laughed together, the bond deepening between them, and both thought that life was now going to be better.

CHAPTER 6

Secrecy, and Dr Crofton

Howard was keen to help his sister find a good doctor who would look after her throughout her pregnancy. A friend of his at the Bombay Railway Institute told him about a British doctor, Daniel Crofton, resident in Bombay. The doctor, a widower in his mid-fifties, had worked in Bombay for many years, only returning to England for his two months' annual leave each year. A committed Christian, a member of the Plymouth Brethren, he believed God had called him to work in India. Margaret was at first reluctant to see him, but eventually she realised she would need to see a doctor regularly to ensure that her baby was healthy. When she went to see him for the first time she was relieved to find him to be a gentle, kind and sympathetic man. On a whim she decided to tell him the whole story, and he listened without interrupting until she had finished. He then spoke to her with the utmost understanding.

Dr Crofton's wife had died three years earlier and his only daughter, Joyce, similar in age to Margaret, lived in Worthing in England. He was often lonely, so would sometimes drop by for a chat with Margaret in between seeing his patients. He became fond of the young woman and took particular care to see she had all she needed to keep herself fit and well. Margaret was convinced he did not charge her the full price for her monthly check-ups and she found him to be a calming influence. He arranged for her baby to be delivered at one of the Catholic hospitals in Bombay, as he felt the care there was second to none. He took

Margaret to visit the hospital so that she could be familiar with it before the birth, and he did not reveal her true story to anyone there or anyone else. Since the hospital was accustomed to looking after people with all sorts of complicated backgrounds and problems, they had no difficulty in accepting that Margaret was a widow, and they made little reference to it. The hospital was a cheerful place, the nurses there were compassionate and, on hearing she was a young widow, they made a special effort to be sympathetic towards her.

Margaret wished her mother was with her, and yet she dreaded how she would have reacted had she known the truth; and she missed the hills in Darjeeling, where it was cool and quiet. Howard immediately told anyone they came across that his sister was a widow – they had settled on the name of Mrs Curzon – and everybody accepted this story without question, but Margaret invariably felt awkward when people called her by this name. No one doubted that she had lost her husband, and Howard and Dr Crofton were the only people who knew the truth. Yet whenever anyone mentioned her 'dead' husband, Margaret experienced considerable unease in sticking to the story of how he had died and repeatedly asked Howard what she should say about this.

'Just say he was having a routine hernia operation and when he woke up from the anaesthetic he had a heart attack. It was completely unexpected. The staff at the British hospital in Darjeeling tried everything they could to save him, but he died an hour after coming round.'

Margaret tried to remember all this, but it did not come naturally to her, and she tried her best to avoid talking about it. When Howard was with her it was so much easier, as he took over and did the talking. He would explain: 'It was an unfortunate medical occurrence after a simple routine operation.'

And to Margaret he was firm, saying: 'If anyone brings the subject up, just say that you prefer not to talk about it, and be careful not to give any specific details.'

The fear of saying the wrong thing terrified Margaret; it was uppermost in her mind and she constantly imagined that people were looking straight through her, knowing she was having an illegitimate child. Daily, she tortured herself by brooding over whether she could ever keep it a secret, let alone keep it a secret for the rest of her life.

In the end it was her childminding job that was her saviour, as it took her mind off her present situation. Although she barely saw Rosalind Grant and her husband, they took pains to let her know how much they valued her care of their two cherished children. Margaret's experience with her younger brothers had given her an unusual insight into the minds of young children, and an awareness of what keeps them happy. It was rare for either of the children to cry or scream, and Margaret kept them quiet, occupied and content. Both the children loved her, and the servants must have told the Grants this, as they were exceptionally appreciative of Margaret. This meant a lot to her, as she knew she was doing something that was important to them and she was also earning money.

Apart from the constant fear that people would discover her true circumstances, Margaret appreciated the fact that her childminding job provided a structure to her day. During the last two months of her pregnancy she found she got more tired, and bitter feelings started to rise as she relived what had taken place between her and Gordon McCall. How deceitful it had been of him not to have told her he was married, and why had he been so kind and loving to her until the moment he heard she was having a baby? Every day she recalled the moment she had told him, and how aghast he had been, how he had avoided looking at her directly, and finally made it clear that he would never acknowledge the child. His assumption that she would have an abortion was another concern of Margaret's, as, from the moment she had discovered she was pregnant, the idea of having an abortion was out of the question. Howard's plan to take her with him to Bombay had been a godsend. Indeed, Margaret asked herself frequently what she would have done without his help.

But it was Dr Crofton who provided the solid rock that Margaret could depend on. He visited her regularly, usually in the mornings when Howard was at work and he knew she would be alone. His visits came to mean a great deal to her and, despite inevitable negative feelings, Margaret felt happier than she had done for some months. She felt she could look forward to having the baby – it would be her own child – and she felt how satisfying it would be to have someone she could be close to, someone who belonged only to her, that no one could take away. During the final weeks of her pregnancy she imagined holding her baby and caring for it. One evening she smiled at Howard and said: 'Thank you for all you've done for me – bringing me here, getting me work, letting me share your apartment. I do feel better now and I can really say I'm looking forward to having my baby; it will be marvellous to have someone of my very own who belongs to me in such a special way.'

They had never discussed whether Margaret would keep the baby or not, and on hearing this Howard was clearly aghast and could not help staring at her in amazement. He responded in a rather brusque manner: 'Darling, you surely didn't think you could bring up a child alone, a British lady in India, with no husband and no money? You must have realised you'll have to give the baby away for adoption once it's born?'

Margaret, dumbfounded, replied: 'Of course I want to keep the baby, Howard. I have always felt this. Now it's getting near to his or her birth I feel this even more strongly; my baby is already part of me, and I would like to bring him or her up myself.'

'You must realise, Margaret, that you cannot possibly do this; you will have no money, and nowhere to live. You must remember too that Nora and I are getting married in six months' time, and you are not going to be able to continue living with me after that,' responded Howard.

Margaret was shocked; she had not thought any further than the birth of her baby, and she had given no consideration whatever to the practical or financial aspects of how she would manage afterwards. This was not entirely her fault, as she'd been brought up with little need to consider the practical side of domesticity. She had very little understanding that with no husband to earn money she would have no way of paying for a place in which to live nor the money necessary to feed and clothe herself and her baby. She slowly came to recognise that once she had the baby she would not be capable of doing any work and as her family were expecting her home about the time of the birth she could not ask them for more money.

Margaret's education at the Loreto Convent, a Catholic institution in Darjeeling commissioned in 1841 by Scottish missionaries, had been exceptional and she was able to hold her own intellectually and talk intelligently on many topics. The convent had a vast library and all the white students took the British Cambridge exams. But it was not accepted for someone with her background and education to go out to work. White women in the 1920s in India were responsible solely for managing the servants and seeing the home ran smoothly – more of an organisational task than a practical one, as the Indian servants saw to all the everyday work.

It took a while for Margaret to fully comprehend that she must find a life away from Howard's and it was the first time she had fully understood that his upcoming marriage to Nora would prevent her from continuing to live with him once he was married. When she realised what her future might be she was aghast. All she wanted was to have her baby and live contentedly with him or her. It took some time for her to accept that Howard was right in insisting she should give the baby away. She had tried so hard to believe she could keep her child, but she realised that if she continued to live in Bombay her story of being a widow might eventually find its way to Darjeeling, and then the truth would come out. Returning to Darjeeling and her family was, of course, a possibility, yet Margaret flinched at this, knowing that she would not be able to take the baby with her. The thought of giving her baby away and then returning to her family and forever hiding her secret was not an option. No, this was not an option – she would not be able to do it.

Thinking of her family reminded her that she should write another letter to her parents to let them know she was well and enjoying life in Bombay. Her previous letters had been difficult to write, as she had had to invent tales of how she was passing her time there. Writing about games, afternoon teas and dances that she had never been to posed a dilemma to Margaret, and endless hours had been spent composing these letters. However, now she decided to tell her parents that she had found a delightful British family who paid her to look after their two young children. They would probably not be thrilled to hear this but she felt that if they knew she was happy, then they would accept it, and it would explain her continued absence from Darjeeling.

As her pregnancy drew to an end, she became more level-headed about the impossibility of bringing up a child on her own in 1920s' India. It took her some time but when she had thought everything through she could see the wisdom of having the baby adopted. But she was heartbroken, and that evening she sobbed and sobbed until she was worn out; finally, she said to Howard: 'I won't be able to keep the baby, *but* I must know that he or she will go to a truly loving British home.'

And Howard, very relieved, replied: 'Good girl. You are doing the right thing; we will find a respectable and trustworthy family to bring up your baby, and then you must recover your natural warm and friendly personality and start a new life. You are still young, you will marry and have more children of your own.'

'Oh Howard, I can't think like that at the moment. The idea of losing my baby is all I can think of now. I can't believe there will be a future for me.'

'Of course there will, darling; you'll put all this behind you and start again and I'm sure you will find a good husband and have more children.'

Margaret was dubious about this but did not say so.

Chapter 7

Birth of Baby Grace, and Heartache

The last few weeks of her pregnancy passed quickly. She said goodbye to the Grants and their children and prepared herself for what was to come. During the final week Dr Crofton called in to see her every day. The good-natured, calm doctor had taken a genuine liking to the young woman, and he understood the agony of what Margaret was going through. He was with her one morning when she went into labour and immediately took her into the quiet and peaceful Catholic hospital. The nursing nuns were kind and gentle and, although they could not take away the brutal agony which racked her body, they cared for Margaret in a loving manner, which made her labour easier. She was never left alone, and her familiar and treasured friend Dr Crofton came in to sit beside her and give her support. She did not know it, but he never left the hospital throughout the night, and finally, just before six in the morning on 23 April 1927, he was with her to deliver her baby.

It was a girl, perfectly formed, with fair skin and fair hair – not Margaret's colouring, much more like Gordon McCall's. But Margaret was so worn out by the agony of giving birth that all she could think of was how she had deceived her family, and how the excruciating suffering of the past eighteen hours would amount to nothing because she would have to give the baby away. She had silently hoped that the baby would be a girl and she took one look at the adorable infant before falling into a deeply troubled sleep. When she woke up two hours later there was a crib beside her with the baby in it. Margaret struggled to sit up, and then peered into the crib. She saw a minute, puckered face with closed eyes, and she knew in that moment that if she once wavered in her decision to let the baby go she would be lost. The one thing that gave her a little strength was that she wanted Grace, as she had named her, to be brought up with a family who could give her a chance of a happy and worthwhile life. The next few days passed in a blur; at one minute Margaret wanted to let Grace go so that the child could have a better life, but the next minute she had surges of longing to keep her. This swinging from one decision to another lasted until the final decision was made quite suddenly on the fourth morning after the birth. Matron came around as usual to see how Grace and Margaret were doing and said casually: 'You are looking better today, Margaret, and I can see that baby Grace is thriving. A British couple from Jubbulpore have been in touch with us; he is a senior administrator in customs there. They have been waiting a long time to adopt a white baby girl and when we told them about Grace they immediately travelled several hours overnight to meet her here.'

Margaret had come to terms with her decision to have Grace adopted, as then the baby would have two proper parents and the chance of a much better future. So, she responded: 'Please take Grace so that they can meet her, and if they feel they really do want her, I think they should have her.'

So tiny Grace was taken to the couple and her lovely soft skin and huge, blue-green eyes charmed them. When they heard that Margaret had named her baby Grace, they promised they would continue to call her this, and then asked if they could take her home with them at once to avoid the need for another long journey. Matron came into Margaret's room and asked her about this: 'I know it will be hard for you, Margaret, but the couple are delighted with Grace, and they would like to take her now if this is all right with you?'

Margaret felt numb and her lips went rigid, but she replied: 'What is the point of hanging onto Grace any longer? It will only make the separation worse for me. Tell them they can have her and ask them to be sure to give her a good life.'

Grace was then brought in so that Margaret could say goodbye to her. As she held her daughter in her arms for one last time, she was racked with anguish. She kissed Grace and told her how she would think of her every day and would always love her, and then she passed the baby back to Matron. Matron had not suggested that Margaret should meet the couple, and for a reason she did not understand herself at the time Margaret did not ask to meet them. It was enough that Matron had said they were good people and were well off financially. As soon as she had said goodbye to Grace, Margaret started to pack her things – she wanted to leave the hospital as soon as she could. Matron came in with a number of papers for Margaret to sign, signifying that she had given Grace away to this British couple and she would not claim her back. Once they were signed, Matron phoned Dr Crofton, and when he had finished his clinic he came to collect her.

Thoughtful and perceptive man that he was, he took her to his own home for a few days. As a doctor, he lived in a comfortable, roomy house, with several Indian servants. Although she was exhausted, mentally and physically, Margaret was everlastingly grateful for his quiet, comforting presence during that first week. She never ever forgot it. He said little, but was there when she wanted to talk and on the third day she poured out all her feelings, most of which she had kept in check throughout her pregnancy. Tears of bitterness flowed, followed by rage against the situation she found herself in. This flood of emotion exhausted her, but it had been cathartic, and she then felt a little better. After a week, she went back to Howard's apartment, and she knew that she must think about her future. She felt she could neither stay in Bombay nor return to her family in Darjeeling. Added to this was the burden of having to tell everyone the untruth that her baby had been stillborn, having suffered from a wrapped umbilical cord during delivery. Howard had thought this was the best idea, as it was the only way to explain why Margaret had no baby. Yet whenever anyone spoke to her sympathetically about her loss she felt uncertain as to how to reply since she knew full well that baby Grace was alive.

Howard had spoken to Margaret quite compellingly. 'I have already told most of the people we know about the stillbirth, so almost everyone you meet will mention it to you and express great sympathy. Just tell them that you are very, very upset at losing Grace, and then say that you are trying to rebuild your life and would rather not talk about it.'

'I'll try, Howard, but I'd prefer not to see people for the moment.'

'That's all right for a bit,' replied Howard. 'I'll protect you from any visitors, but you must aim to pick up a normal life for someone of your age.'

Still feeling the aftermath of the ordeal she had suffered, Margaret found herself wanting to stay in the apartment and not speak to anyone. Even Howard's houseboy thought the baby had been stillborn and although he was considerate, he kept referring to it, until Margaret told him bluntly not to do so. She was not devious and she hated telling an untruth, but Howard urged her to say what he had told her and no more.

'Darling, they will understand that you don't want to talk about it, so simply leave it there and be careful to say nothing further.'

Margaret tried her best and since anyone speaking to her could see that she was extremely upset, it was no problem for them to accept the news of her stillborn baby, and to appreciate that she was not herself at this time. When kindly women sympathised with her over her loss she would quickly become tearful, but no one suspected what had happened, thinking it was natural for her to be upset. However, despite this, she lived in fear of someone discovering her true story. She was grieving daily over the loss of Grace, but also a bitter remorse haunted her, as she felt she was deceiving all her family and everyone around her, something which made her feel utterly dejected and miserable.

Another complication was Howard's forthcoming marriage. Nora had been very understanding about Howard's sister, but Margaret accepted that once Howard and Nora were married she could not continue to live in Howard's apartment. Since moving back there, Margaret's emotions see-sawed up and down and there seemed no point to her life. Every day she went over the events of the past year – meeting Gordon, falling in love with him, the wonderful times they had had together, thinking about getting married to him. Then discovering she was pregnant and feeling certain he would be delighted and want to get married immediately; seeing his utter dismay at the prospect of a child and, finally, how he almost pushed her away. These recurring thoughts played on her mind not just daily but almost hourly. Besides which she had been calling herself Mrs Curzon since her arrival in Bombay and she had never got used to this and shuddered every time anyone used it.

However, she was young, and she quickly recovered her physical strength. Her body became slim again and eventually she felt slightly more optimistic and decided she would look for some work. But Howard refused to let her take any kind of job, saying it was not in keeping with their family or the type of people he met socially here. He pointed out that her childminding job had only been to help out some friends of his, and it was not fitting for her to be working. He added: 'Now that you are well again I will make a point of letting all my friends and business contacts know that my young widowed sister is staying with me. I am sure this will lead to many invitations, and you must be prepared to get out socially again.'

'Howard, I will try my best, but at the moment I don't feel like venturing out too much,' answered Margaret.

'I know,' replied Howard. 'After what you have been through it will be an effort. But I'm sure you will be invited to one or two things, just see how you get on; I think it will do you good. Remember how we used to have fun as a family when we went out together for games and picnics?'

And Margaret laughed as she remembered the good times the family had enjoyed together.

After a month she was fully aware that she must try to be more outgoing. In fact, this was her natural expressive and warm nature, but it had been obscured by the unexpected turn of events in her life. She tried on some of the clothes she had not worn since being pregnant, as well as the two new dresses her mother had told her to buy before she left Darjeeling. As she looked in the mirror, she saw that she appeared slim, attractive and even alluring. Howard kept his word and made it known that his widowed sister was staying with him, and it was enough for invitations to start to arrive for picnics, soirées, dances and lunches; it made no difference that Margaret was thought to be a widow, in fact it brought sympathy and the wish to help her.

The social life for the British in 1920s' Bombay was similar to that in Darjeeling, except that Bombay was a very much larger city. An underground railway was already proposed, there was a well-regarded University and it was a melting pot of different cultures. Already the principal financial city of India, Bombay was also the scene of swing and jazz, while varied religions and spiritual cults blossomed. Wherever the British lived in the city there were plenty of social groups and clubs, which they made full use of. Leisure, fun, dances, picnics and balls were the norm. Moreover, there were so many young British men in the army and in businesses there that the younger women were much in demand.

The invitations started to flow in to Margaret, but at first her confidence was still low. However, with her new clothes she gradually felt more positive and self-assured. Nora had been very kind too and lent her a couple of stylish dresses for more formal occasions. She also had the small allowance that Howard gave her – he had told her he could only do this until he was married, as he would then need the money to keep his new wife. Margaret understood this and knew she must look for a husband. As her former charm and vivacity returned, it was not long before there were several men who sought her out since, at twenty-four, she was unusually lovely, with deep olive skin, a gently rounded face and completely natural, jet black hair.

Chapter 8

Meeting Edwyn

The stately and imposing structure of the Victorian building that housed the Civil Service Club was one of the main meeting places for the British in Bombay. The many generously proportioned rooms had a welcoming atmosphere and were used for lunches and dinners, and games such as table tennis, billiards and snooker. Snooker had been a popular game in India since the late nineteenth century – invented by an Englishman from Sandhurst who was posted to India in 1875, the game quickly became popular there. Table tennis was also well liked, and Margaret found she was still an excellent table tennis player and within two weeks she was sought after for matches.

'Margaret, could you please come and make up a doubles with us?' was a familiar request.

And Margaret found she was at ease with this uncomplicated way of socialising, and she started to smile and laugh again.

Howard had taken great pains to introduce Margaret to some of his friends and associates, and it had paid off. His wine and spirit business was doing well but was still in its early stages. Being a realistic, down-to-earth man, he was a trifle apprehensive that Margaret might retreat into herself and make little effort to charm the men. However, she was aware that she needed to find a husband, or she would have to go back to her family in Darjeeling. Several men were attracted to the vivacious girl, but as soon as a man became serious Margaret would shy away from him. Howard became a little exasperated with her and told her plainly she must not be so choosy.

There were two young men in particular who were utterly captivated by Margaret and would not take no for an answer – Johnnie Turner-Craig and William Dickson. Both were officers in the British Army and had been introduced to Margaret by a friend of Howard's. Johnnie was somewhat flamboyant and light-hearted and paid Margaret a lot of compliments, but he reminded her of Gordon and she felt he had no depth to him. When Johnnie proposed, Howard urged her to accept him, but Margaret turned him down, as her intuition told her that Johnnie would have no time for her if he knew her true story. William Dickson was also enchanted by her and he was quite different from Johnnie, but he was so quiet and reserved that Margaret felt she would never really get to know him. She quite liked him but when he proposed she hesitated, and after thinking about it for a few days she refused him too, again feeling unsure as to how he would react if he knew her history. Thinking that she might not meet another man, she became tense and anxious, but she felt adamant that she did not want to hide her past from a future husband, feeling it would haunt her all her life if she did.

Howard was none too pleased. 'At the rate you are going you may not get another chance,' he grumbled.

'I'm not going to marry someone unless I feel that I can live with them for the rest of my life,' responded Margaret.

For a while Howard was right. A month went by and even though Margaret led a gay and pleasurable social life she did not collect any more serious suitors. It was now September 1927 and Howard was becoming more and more anxious for her to find a husband. A few days later a Ball was held at the Civil Service Club, to which Margaret was invited. Early in the evening she was introduced to Edwyn Nicholson, a twenty-seven-year-old Australian. Normally reticent and unforthcoming, he had spotted her across the ballroom and asked to be introduced. Edwyn and his brother Hubert had both emigrated to England when Edwyn was eighteen and Hubert twenty, and Edwyn had been fortunate in being able to join the British Civil Service in London just when they were recruiting personnel. He was out in Bombay for nine months, helping to establish the further development of the Civil Service base out there, and had eight more months to serve. Edwyn was an extremely pleasant and gentle person, solid, reliable and stable – qualities that Margaret badly needed. He was somewhat lacking in ambition and drive, and not the most entertaining person – indeed, some of the girls considered him dull, but the friendly and vivacious girl attracted him right away. At his first sight of Margaret she was talking to another man, but he overcame his usual retiring nature to walk over and wait to be introduced to her. Margaret was wearing a long satin dress with a net overskirt in a vivid shade of coral. It was kindly Nora who had lent it to her, and the skirt set off Margaret's slim waist and hips. Edwyn could not take his eyes off her and with Margaret's natural, warm personality he found himself able to talk to her easily. They had several dances together and at the end of the evening he asked if he might call on her the following day. And Margaret felt comfortable in saying yes.

The following day Edwyn called round, and after this they saw each other frequently. They would sit together for hours and talk about their lives, which had been so dissimilar. Margaret was able to draw Edwyn out and he told her about his childhood in Melbourne, Australia, while she told him about her life in Darjeeling. Edwyn became wholly and unreservedly committed to her, drawn to her approachable nature and friendly charm, yet he was able to sense a deeper side to her. Margaret was not in the least in love with Edwyn, but she valued him enormously for his dependability and his obvious devotedness. He was completely different from Gordon McCall, who had been flamboyant and flippant, and she was thankful for this. He was also the first man she had met with whom she felt she might trust her past secrets. He would call round to Howard's apartment whenever he could and they would sit and talk in the garden together, but so far she had not told him about Grace. But Edwyn, in fact, had always felt there was something Margaret had kept from him, and then one afternoon she hesitantly told him about Gordon McCall and baby Grace; he listened to her confidences without interrupting and without being judgmental. When she had finished telling him, he put his arm around her and gave her a gentle hug. He had been deeply touched by her story and he could see how profoundly this experience had affected her. Somehow this drew them closer together. Two days later he called round and asked her if she would marry him when he returned to England. Suddenly it was as if a great weight fell from Margaret and she instantly knew this was the perfect answer to all her problems. She would marry Edwyn and leave India and her past life behind. She would never have to return to Darjeeling and potential shame, and she could start a new, untarnished life in England as a married woman.

Margaret was ecstatic, she did not hesitate for a moment and she responded at once by saying: 'Yes, I will.'

Edwyn drew her close to him and kissed her; he was overjoyed, his happiness was complete. He had listened to her story about Gordon McCall and baby Grace, and instantly believed she had been taken in by a fast-talking, married man, which of course she had. Margaret wanted to write at once to her mother to tell her the good news about the engagement – it was now getting on for a year since she had left Darjeeling. Throughout that year she had written only intermittently to her; it had required a big effort on her part to indicate she was having a good time but also to hide her pregnancy. When baby Grace was born she had longed to tell her mother, knowing how pleased she would be with another grandchild, but of course she could not have told her the circumstances.

Now she could write and tell her all about Edwyn, how they had met, how kind and gentle he was and how happy she was to have found him. The one drawback was that she would be moving to England and would be far away from her family. She said she would have loved to have seen them all before she moved to England, but there was no time – the only ship sailing there in the next few months left in three weeks' time, and she needed to take this passage to prepare for her wedding. The journey to and from Darjeeling would take six days and a visit was going to be impossible in the time available. The family, though very disappointed they would not be seeing Margaret before she left Bombay, were thrilled at her news and they just had time to reply before she sailed. Margaret's relief at being able to move to England without letting anything slip about Gordon or baby Grace was immense. She shuddered at the thought of her family knowing her true story.

Howard was delighted at the engagement. He knew all too well what his sister had been through and he wanted the best for her, so her engagement to Edwyn seemed just the right thing to him. In fact, it was a load off his shoulders since he had wondered what would happen to her had she not married. And the fact that Edwyn lived in England was the perfect answer, as she would never have to explain about Grace to their parents and friends in Darjeeling. Howard winced at the thought of this. Had Margaret chosen to remain in Bombay, it was highly likely that the story of the baby would at some point have reached their parents. The

Indian railway system was fast developing and there would always have been the fear that at some point her story would have leaked out. On top of this Howard wanted to get married to Nora as soon as possible and Nora was understandably getting impatient. Once they were married there would be no room in his apartment for Margaret and so he willingly did all he could to help Margaret and Edwyn make arrangements for a passage on the SS *Ragnera*, the next ship going to England. Now that he had met Edwyn, he saw that he was just starting out in his career, and it seemed to Howard that although Edwyn was an agreeable and laid back person, he was unambitious and might stay at the same level in the Civil Service for some years. Bearing this in mind and guessing that Edwyn would be hard-pressed to find the money for Margaret's passage to England, Howard paid for it, albeit only in a third-class cabin. Margaret immediately applied for a passport and was relieved to find there was not too much of a delay in issuing it since the authorities were used to the British sailing back and forth to Britain.

It was now that Margaret came to appreciate all that Howard had done for her. If it had not been for him she might have had to tell her parents and her other brothers about her pregnancy or, worse still, go to an Indian abortionist and possibly be ill-treated there. The thought of this had been unthinkable to her, and it made her more and more thankful to Howard, not only for keeping her secret to himself but also for seeing she was looked after throughout these difficult months. Nora had been a good friend, no doubt because she was aware how fortunate she was to have met Howard and to be getting married to him in the traditional way. She was genuinely delighted that Margaret had eventually found a man who would marry and care for her and, above all, that she could leave India and her past behind her. Margaret was in tears when she thanked Nora for supporting her at bad times, and for being such a good solid friend; Nora too knew they had formed a strong bond and she was genuinely sad to be losing Margaret. Margaret made a point of specifically showing her appreciation to her brother, and when she spoke her voice shook as she said: 'Howard, you have been there for me throughout this troublesome time in my life and taken care of me during it all. I cannot tell you how much this has meant to me.'

Howard, a stable and decent type of man, smiled and was thankful he had helped her, and replied: 'Things have finally turned out for the best for you, little sister. Meeting Edwyn here has been good for you, as it means you can start a new life in England and forget the regrettable relationship with Gordon. You'll be married and I hope you will have more children, children who will be yours to keep and nurture.'

The relief to them both was apparent, as the fear that Margaret's story would in time be known here in Bombay and then in Darjeeling had disturbed them equally.

Edwyn would return to London in May 1928, and Margaret was to go ahead on the ship to arrange the marriage and find them somewhere to live. While she waited for the sailing date, Margaret spent as much time with Edwyn as she could. He clearly adored her and was ready to show his feelings towards her, always complimenting her on how she looked, and it was evident to everyone around them how deeply in love he was with her. As Edwyn had always been a rather reserved person, his work companions were surprised at how much he had come out of his shell and how much more he was now able to express his emotions to other people. Margaret felt a little overwhelmed by his constant affection towards her, as she was not desperately in love with him; rather, she felt an enormous sense of gratitude that through him she would be able to leave her past behind her and start a new life in England. Edwyn had made sure that Margaret had somewhere to stay in England – she would go to his aunt and uncle in Beckenham, Kent, and his brother Hubert would also look after her. Edwyn and Hubert shared a small flat, also in Beckenham. He knew he could depend on them all to welcome Margaret and that they would do all they could to help her make the transition to the British way of life.

Making this shift to England was known to be difficult for the Anglo-Indians. Their life in India had accustomed them to live without the encumbrance of household duties of any kind, these being taken care of by their Indian servants. When they returned to England, they experienced a significant shock – suddenly the domestic matters and household chores now all fell on them. On top of this was the necessity to adapt to a different country's way of living. The shops in India were eye-catching and adorned with brightly coloured scarves and materials, and the various types of food were often mixed up in the same shop. In England the shops seemed colourless and were not nearly as exotic. Additionally, anyone coming to live in England who was used to the heat of India had a sudden shock when they arrived to find the damp and wet climate, and the cold and icy winters were especially intolerable to them.

Edwyn spent much of his spare time trying to do his best to prepare Margaret for her move to England, yet nothing could prepare an Anglo-Indian for the immense change between the two countries. As Margaret was so exhilarated by the thought of leaving India and her past totally behind, she was not able to take in much of what Edwyn told her. Her only real friends in Bombay were Howard and Nora, the Grants and Dr Crofton. At such a traumatic time in her life these few friends had all meant so much to her and she was loath to leave them.

Dr Crofton had been her rock of Gibraltar and she particularly remembered how kind he had been. He had supported her while she was expecting Grace and given her encouragement as she slowly built her life up again after the birth. The good doctor had been deeply moved by the plight of the young woman and promised that when he was back in England for his two months' annual leave he would come and see her; as well as this, he had written to his daughter, Joyce, in Worthing, and asked her to both phone and write to Margaret. He felt sure that Margaret and Joyce would become good friends – they were of a similar age and she was also a member of the Plymouth Brethren. The only other friends Margaret had were the Grant family, whose two young children she had looked after when she was expecting her baby. However, since they did not know her full story and believed her baby had been stillborn, Margaret always felt a certain reserve when she met them, as she had to be guarded about anything that might hint at her past situation.

The time came for the ship to sail. Howard, Nora, Dr Crofton and, of course, Edwyn all came to see her off. The passenger steamship SS *Ragnera* was in the Bombay dock, people were going on board and goodbyes were being said. Edwyn was obviously particularly affected by the parting, and Margaret was very apprehensive about facing the voyage alone but they all hugged and kissed her and she embarked. As the ship set off for Tilbury docks, they waved at her until she was out of sight. She was heartened by knowing it would not be too long before Edwyn would be coming back to England and they would be together again, but as the ship slowly moved away and she lost sight of her Bombay 'family', she suddenly felt horribly deserted and feelings of remorse yet again flooded over her.

Chapter 9

The SS Ragnera, and Ben

The SS *Ragnera* gradually gathered speed and Margaret watched the city of Bombay fade into the distance. Before long there was nothing but the sound of waves lashing against the sides of the ship. She made her way to her cabin and was dismayed to find it was a very small inside cabin, from where she had no view of the outside world. It felt airless and oppressive, so she unpacked the clothes she would need for the passage and went onto the decks reserved for tourist class passengers. In the 1920s a strict class structure was in operation on board, according to the price paid for the journey. Tourist class passengers took their meals in a far less superior restaurant than the first or second class passengers. The first class cabins were large and splendidly decorated and these were taken by the more notable people, such as judges and colonial statesmen.

Margaret spent the next few days getting accustomed to the noise and smell of the ship and its routine, and as she did not have much appetite she ate very little. The crew were all Indian and the tourist class restaurant was equipped with only basic tables and chairs; Margaret found they reminded her of her school dining room. Most of the other passengers were considerably older than her, and she made little effort to speak to them. What also held her back was having to be careful to only mention that she was engaged to Edwyn, and to refrain from being tempted to let out anything further about her past life.

She investigated more of the ship and found a smoking room and a writing room. The latter was a quiet place for passengers to write letters or cards or to read their books. There was also a room set aside as a chapel, and the padre was available to give help, advice or spiritual comfort. On Sundays two church services were held, an Anglican one and a Roman Catholic one, with sherry served after each service. But Margaret did not go to either service; the whole ordeal of baby Grace had left her Catholic faith shattered.

She had soon explored all the areas where tourist class passengers were allowed and they were not especially pleasant. Returning to her small, stuffy cabin did not help and she grew disheartened. However, on the fourth day of the voyage she stumbled upon the games section, a large and more pleasing area, which was common to all passengers. Here she found table tennis tables, deck quoits, a snooker table, a number of tables for card games and a swimming pool. After hesitating, Margaret went and sat quietly and watched people making use of the variety of sports offered. She would have loved to join in but felt intimidated by the huge ship and having to cope on her own, so after a while she left. But the following day she returned to the games section and found herself more at ease to speak with one or two people. A game of deck quoits was taking place and a lady asked her if she would make up a team for a friendly match they were having. Margaret jumped up at once and joined the team. It turned out to be good fun and allowed her to speak to several other people without feeling uncomfortable.

After this Margaret went to the games section every day and began to be more at ease with those around her. She joined in playing deck quoits and table tennis. The other passengers were happy to include the lovely young woman in their games, and her skill at table tennis quickly became apparent. She found her confidence increased and this proved to be the one thing that made her life on board less lonely. As the days went by, Margaret felt more self-assured and she chatted happily to those around her. By now she had become a welcome and popular young lady. A week into the voyage she found a table tennis tournament had been arranged, and she put her name down for it. Thirty-two people had entered and the tournament drew a lot of interest even from the non-players. After the first round, sixteen players were left, and after the second round eight remained. Margaret was still in the tournament and had easily beaten both her opponents. It was now the semi-final and Margaret's opponent was a man who was a good player and considerably better than her two previous competitors. Yet she won the match without too much opposition. Surprised to find she was in the final, Margaret was determined to win the tournament. She forgot all about her past troubles and set her mind on the task. Her fellow finalist was an older woman and Margaret could see she was also determined to win. After a tough battle, when Margaret forced herself to concentrate on every point, she was delighted to find that she was the winner. Lots of congratulations followed and Margaret started to feel she had made her mark on many of the other passengers on the ship.

The passengers were divided between those who spent their time in a deck chair sitting in the sun, and those who felt a bit of exercise and socialising was a good thing. Winning the table tennis tournament had given Margaret a certain standing with the other passengers and she was often asked to join in with a number of the other games. Her self-assurance grew.

One afternoon she signed up to play deck quoits and found she was partnered with a rather debonair older man in his fifties, whom she had not met before. He introduced himself saying: 'Hello, I'm Ben Charlton. I haven't seen you before, where did you get on the ship?' Margaret replied: 'I got on in Bombay. I'm Margaret Horton, how do you do?'

They played three games together, during which they learnt more of each other. Ben told her that he was a widower. 'I have recently sold my business and have been out to Australia and am now travelling back home to England. I live in London.'

'Oh,' said Margaret, 'I'm going to London too. I'm engaged to Edwyn, an Australian I met in Bombay while I was staying with my brother.'

'You are travelling alone?' he enquired.

'I am, but I'll be making my way to an address just outside London where my fiancé's brother lives.'

Ben was interested and continued to tell Margaret a bit more about himself. 'I had a wine and spirit business for many years until I recently sold it, which has allowed me to travel in comfort wherever and whenever I like.'

Margaret told him about her brother Howard's wine and spirit business and they chatted for a few minutes.

Ben was courteous, distinguished and, one would almost say, dashing. He had always wanted to go out to Australia so had gone there by ship and travelled around the vast country; now he was going back to his home in Wilbraham Place, London. None of this meant a great deal to Margaret, as he was talking of a world she knew little of. She listened to his tales of where he had been in Australia – the wonderful beaches, the hot climate in the north of the country, and the magnificent cities of Sydney, Brisbane, Melbourne, Perth and Adelaide. Ben had visited them all. She found she was able to tell him of her life in Darjeeling and managed to say how she had met Edwyn, her fiancé, while staying with her brother in Bombay without mentioning anything about Grace. After their first meeting she often found Ben in the games section of the ship. He had been lonely since his wife had died and he felt a certain compassion for the young woman who was going to have to make a new life in England. Margaret came to look on him as a kind and benevolent uncle, and as he was travelling first class and obviously wealthy and well-to-do she felt particularly safe when she was with him. She talked to him more about her engagement to Edwyn and how she would need to travel to London, where Edwyn's brother was to meet her and take her to his aunt and uncle's in Beckenham. Ben asked how she was getting to London and she told him she was going by train. Ben had a car meeting him at Tilbury and knowing that Margaret was travelling alone he offered to take her to where Edwyn's aunt and uncle lived. Margaret, who was not of a practical nature, had been worried about getting from Tilbury to London, where Hubert would meet her, and she accepted his offer gratefully and realised how lucky she was to have met him.

Ben, being very much a man of the world and well travelled, could see that Margaret was unaccustomed to travelling alone, and knowing the comfortable lifestyle of white people in India he could see she was going to find it hard to adapt to the completely different culture in England. He was aware of how demanding this would be for Margaret, and he saw that she was not naturally down-to-earth, but more pensive and thoughtful. First class passengers were allowed to invite the other classes into their social areas, and he decided to invite her into these and also to have her meals in the first class restaurant with him. Margaret noticed a big difference here – the food was significantly superior, the décor of the restaurant was so much more chic and stylish, and the passengers ensured they were well-dressed for dinner. After dinner, dancing took place in a specially reserved area. Margaret made sure she was dressed elegantly for dinner each night and thought how lucky she was to have been invited into the first class accommodation; and knowing that Ben would take her direct to Edwyn's aunt and uncle once the ship had arrived in Tilbury, her mood lifted and her vivacity and warm-heartedness returned.

The ship sailed past Aden and negotiated the Suez Canal. At the far end they could see the octagonal lighthouse at Port Said from where directions were given to ensure that each ship went safely through. The canal at this time was 102 miles long and a vital short cut between the Red Sea and the Mediterranean Sea and, as the ship went through, Margaret noticed that one could almost touch its sides.

When they arrived at the natural harbour of the city of Port Said, everyone was keen to disembark and thankful to get off the ship. By then a genuine friendship had developed between the rather lonely older man and the younger woman. Margaret would never have left the ship on her own, as she would have been terrified to step into an unknown place, but Ben had no fear of this. He took her with him and ordered a taxi and a guide to take them to see something of the city. As they were driven around, they saw many buildings built in the Egyptian style, some of them comparatively new. The city had several Bahá'í temples (which taught the essential worth of all religions), and, of course, the octagonal lighthouse, which they had seen from afar. It had been built in 1869, just before the opening of the Suez Canal, using a novel building technique, including reinforced concrete. Margaret was delighted to see the city and be taken around it in comfort. Ben proposed that they have lunch at a local restaurant and, after looking at the menu, he said: 'I have been to Egypt before and I know the type of food they eat here. You probably won't recognise much of the items on the menu. Would you like to try some fava beans, baklava and *om ali*, they are typical Egyptian foods?'

'I would love to try them,' replied Margaret, and so they were ordered, plus lentils, which Margaret was already familiar with.

'This is delicious,' she said, 'and the *om ali* reminds me of a type of bread pudding.'

'That is just what it is,' replied Ben. 'Eat as much as you like.'

Margaret was obviously entranced by the whole day and the delicious lunch, and Ben was touched to see her unaffected happiness, noticing a certain naiveté in her.

Now in the Mediterranean, the ship slowly passed the southern tip of Sicily and sailed north to Marseille, where they would be spending the day. It was springtime and warm, although not as warm as Margaret was used to and she was conscious of a cooler climate. Again, Ben hired a taxi and a guide and they toured the city, seeing the recently re-built opera house, as well as the many buildings in French-style architecture and the nearly completed Rove tunnel, which connected the city to the river Rhône. It was a major work of civil engineering and one of the longest such tunnels in France. The French influence and lifestyle charmed Margaret, and she especially loved the cafés, where people sat outside drinking coffee and watching the world go by. Ben suggested they stop for lunch at one of the bistros and he introduced her to French cuisine.

'Why not order mussels in wine and shallots?' he said. Margaret let herself be guided by him, and she loved the mussels served in this way.

'For dessert why not try the *gaufres* – they're a type of waffle, with strawberries and *petit suisse*, which is like a light cream cheese enriched with cream,' recommended Ben.

Margaret let herself be advised by the well-travelled, kindly older man, and after eating all these new foods she told Ben: 'That was absolutely delectable, Ben; thank you for such a lovely meal and for advising me so well.'

This kind of food was completely new to Margaret since her family, as third-generation Anglo-Indians, had very much adapted to the Indian way of eating. Although they ate British food a lot of the time, they had become accustomed to the Indian spices as well and tended to add them liberally to their food. The French attitude to food in valuing delicate and exquisite flavours rather than quantity was particularly attractive to Margaret, so much so that her first visit to France stayed in her mind all her life.

From Marseille the ship continued down the eastern coast of Spain and passed the British overseas territory of Gibraltar. The huge rock of the island was easily seen from the ship, and a glimpse was had of the resident colony of Barbary apes. From there they sailed up the west coast of Portugal and into the Bay of Biscay, on the west coast of France, renowned for its stormy and turbulent seas – fog and windstorms could happen at any time of the year and it was known that ship passengers were frequently badly seasick. True to form, severe weather meant that Margaret and many of the passengers felt unwell and kept to their cabins, while Ben, a seasoned traveller, was not affected and stayed on deck. By the time the ship had passed through the Bay and into the English Channel, however, Margaret had completely recovered and was out on deck as they passed the islands of Jersey and Guernsey. From there the ship made its way slowly around the south-east corner of England and Margaret had her first sight of the country in which she was going to live. She peered and peered at the passing towns and countryside, trying to imagine how life would be there.

Ben reassured Margaret that he had a car meeting him at Tilbury, which would take her to Beckenham, Kent, a town about twelve miles south-east of London, where Edwyn's aunt and uncle lived. She was greatly relieved to know she would not be left alone once they disembarked. By the time Tilbury was in sight, the final stop in the long voyage, Margaret was hovering between excitement and anxiety. As the ship made its leisurely way up the River Thames into the docks at dawn, all she could see were tall, dark, depressing buildings. As they disembarked, the rain was pouring down and Margaret felt rather chilly; she had not taken many warm clothes to Bombay and had not thought to buy any before she left.

Passengers were jostling to get off the ship, so Margaret made sure she stayed very close to Ben. As soon as they were on land, he knew exactly in which direction to go to find the cars that were meeting the passengers, but with the rain and chilly atmosphere, Margaret found she was rather dismayed at her first sight of her new homeland.

Chapter 10

The Rolls Royce

Edwyn had given Margaret the phone number of Bertha and Walter, his aunt and uncle, and told her to phone them from a phone box when she knew what time the train from Tilbury would arrive at Fenchurch Street station. They would let Edwyn's brother Hubert know and he would meet her there. Of course, Margaret had never seen a British phone box before and had no idea how to find one or how they worked. Ben, however, had no trouble finding a porter, who put their luggage on a trolley and wheeled it towards the long line of waiting cars. As they walked along in the rain and cold, they passed a row of three phone boxes and Ben made the phone call. He got through straight away to Bertha and told her that he had met Margaret on the ship and, as he had a car waiting for him, he would bring her directly to their address. Bertha was mightily relieved to speak to him and to hear that Margaret had arrived safely in England. Ben made a note of their address and hung up.

'All is well, Margaret,' Ben told her. 'I have explained how we met on the ship from Bombay, and that I'm driving you to their house. Bertha is going to phone Hubert to let him know that he'll not need to meet you at Fenchurch Street.'

'What a relief,' said Margaret, 'to have made contact with them. Since I know no one in England, I'll be depending on them a lot.'

Ben looked at her. 'It's going to mean a great adjustment for you to change your life to another culture, Margaret. I know Edwyn spent a lot of time telling you about life here, but even so, you are probably not prepared for the immense difference in the way the British live – after all, you have spent the whole of your life living in India. This is another continent and quite another culture.'

Ben was worried – he had previously seen her innocence and lack of worldly knowledge and he wondered how she would cope with her new life.

Margaret was looking at the long line of cars waiting to claim passengers from the ship, but she had no idea what type of car Ben owned. To her amazement, Ben then signalled to a Rolls Royce limousine with a chauffeur in uniform who was waiting for them. She was completely taken aback, as this luxury was not something she was accustomed to. As she got into the gleaming black car, she noticed its polished wooden fitments and the glass partition that separated the passengers from the chauffeur. In the passenger compartment, two pull-down seats faced the soft beige suede, three-seater back seat. Ben greeted the chauffeur and explained that they would be dropping Margaret off at an address in Beckenham, Kent. The chauffeur acknowledged Margaret by saying: 'Hello, Miss. You must be tired and cold. I have the heating turned on in the car.'

'Oh, thank you. It is certainly not very warm here,' she replied.

'My first impressions are not very pleasant,' she thought, 'but I'm sure the damp and cold will improve.'

Ben was totally at ease in the luxurious car and he did his best to make Margaret feel at ease too. The chauffeur, Clarkson, piled their luggage into the roomy boot and they drove off. Ben spoke to Clarkson through a device rather like a miniature loudspeaker and instructed him to head for Beckenham, turning off at Sidcup rather than going directly to London. As the Rolls purred along, Margaret tried to accustom herself to this luxury and take in everything that was passing. Ben pointed out certain buildings, including the new hospital in Tilbury that had been opened by the Duke of York only three years previously. As they passed neat rows of houses in the town, Margaret noticed how unlike these were to the houses she was used to in Darjeeling, or indeed in Bombay, where houses were often dotted around haphazardly. The landscape also appeared strange to her – it was April and the rain was still pouring down but the one saving grace was that the heating system in the Rolls was working and the inside of the car was warm.

Although Margaret had expected to meet Hubert at Fenchurch Street station, she was extremely thankful that she had not had to do this. Edwyn had told her that he and his brother Hubert shared a very small flat on the top floor of a house in Beckenham, not too far from his aunt and uncle. He said that when they were married they would not be able to live there since, even if Hubert moved out, the flat was minute and on the third floor. Margaret had no idea what size a small flat in England could be, as even Howard's apartment in Bombay had reasonably sized rooms.

The Rolls continued smoothly on its way and soon crossed the River Thames and passed through Dartford. Although Edwyn had shown Margaret a number of photos, she knew little of what to expect in England, mainly because it had never crossed her mind that she would ever go there. She hoped the rain would stop soon so she could get a clearer view of the countryside around her. After Dartford, the landscape became less rural and more built up. They finally arrived in Beckenham and found Bertha and Walter's house. Ben wanted to make quite sure that Margaret was at the right place and so he knocked at the door. A cheerful, middle-aged lady opened it and said: 'Come right in, both of you. You must be so tired and hungry; what a nasty day. You're Ben, of course; we spoke on the phone. And who is that outside? Oh, he's your chauffeur? He must be tired and hungry too. What a good idea to have phoned me, I have just put a meat pie in the oven.'

She gave Margaret a kiss and called up the stairs to her husband. 'Walter, Margaret has arrived and she's with her friend from the ship who has brought her here. Can you come down?'

By now they were all sitting in the lounge and Edwyn's uncle Walter joined them. A quiet but kindly man, he smiled at Margaret, gave her a hug, and said: 'Hello, Margaret, how lovely to meet you at last. Edwyn has told us so much about you, we feel we know you already. And we are so pleased you'll be living with us until you get married.'

He welcomed Ben, and then through the window he noticed the Rolls Royce parked there. He was speechless but decided to say nothing and find out later how Margaret had come to be in the company of a man with a sumptuous car like this.

Ben explained how he and Margaret had met on the SS *Ragnera*; then, confident of her welcome into the home, he said he would be on his way. But Bertha insisted he had some hot tea and cake, while the meat pie was cooking, and she would give his chauffeur the same in the kitchen. She pressed Ben to stay for a late lunch, but he just accepted some tea and cake for himself and for Clarkson. Margaret reminded him that she needed to look around for a place for Edwyn and her to live in once they were married. Ben smiled to himself, as he could not see Margaret, totally inexperienced in the ways of British culture as she was, going around house agents and asking for particulars.

'Don't worry,' he told her. 'I'll get in touch with a few agents for you and see what is on the market at the moment. Edwyn has told you what he can afford.'

'Oh, Ben, thank you so much. I would have no idea how to set about doing this,' she replied.

'I'll phone you once I have some particulars, and I'll take you in the car to see the places; you won't be able to manage on your own.'

Having said this and after telling Margaret that he would come back when he had found some property details, he headed off in the Rolls for central London. Despite the warm welcome she was having from Edwyn's aunt and uncle, Margaret felt out of place and uneasy in a house that was so unlike anything she had been used to in India. She missed Howard and her other friends in Bombay and felt that Ben was the only person she had any real connection with.

As soon as Ben and Clarkson had gone, Bertha asked Margaret how she had managed to meet a man like Ben, a man with a Rolls Royce and a chauffeur! Margaret explained how their paths had crossed on the ship and how kind the older man had been to her. Both Walter and Bertha were relieved that Ben would take over the search for a place in which Edwyn and Margaret would live. They were a simple, homely couple who had lived in the same small, semi-detached house since they had emigrated to England, from Australia, in their early twenties. Thankful to have found a small home, they had lived there modestly for thirty years and were happy with their unpretentious life. They were genuinely glad to have Margaret living with them for the next few months, and Margaret could see they were both making an effort to see that she settled in.

The house was infinitely smaller than Margaret's home in Darjeeling, but Bertha had made one of the three upstairs bedrooms into a room for

Margaret. She had put fresh flowers in there and an armchair, for Margaret to sit in and read or write, and tried to make it comfortable for her. The rooms were not spacious, they were simple but had a cosy feel. Margaret looked around the house and at the furniture, which seemed so heavy and solid compared to that in her home in India. There, possessions tended to be plain and unadorned, while here the furniture appeared dark and almost cumbersome; the place felt a bit depressing to Margaret.

Bertha, Walter and Margaret sat down to eat the meat pie, followed by apple crumble. Margaret was hungry and pleased to be given something to eat. Bertha was a basic cook but she took pains to make meals a pleasurable time. After finishing her meal Margaret felt a bit disorientated. She had used up a lot of energy trying to take in her new country on the journey from Tilbury; then making an effort to feel at home in a house that felt strange to her had left her wanting desperately to get to bed even though it was still early. Bertha took her to her room, telling her to only unpack what was necessary for the night, and not to worry about what time she got up in the morning.

Margaret fell deeply asleep and did not wake up until ten o'clock the next morning. Gazing out of her bedroom window she could not see a great deal, as there was a grey mist shrouding everything. As she went downstairs the house did not feel warm, even though Bertha assured her there were radiators in most of the rooms. While they had breakfast, Bertha talked to Margaret about the town of Beckenham and said she would take her around and show her the shops. The town had grown over recent years and was now a popular location for people who needed to travel daily to London for work – the train service was every half-hour throughout the day. Before going to India, Edwyn had been doing this ever since he had started work with the Civil Service. Margaret tried to listen carefully and take in what Bertha was saying to her, but the transition to another continent, so dissimilar from India, made it hard to concentrate. Bertha understood and suggested she spend the day quietly unpacking her trunk, which she did.

The following day Bertha suggested a short walk to the local shops, so that Margaret could get a feel for the area and get to know the shopkeepers. Only five minutes' walk away was a row of stores selling most of the food products needed and other necessities. All the products were neatly arranged in order, so unlike their colourful counterparts in India where one could wander round touching all the wares on show. Each shop sold only a limited selection of food, whereas in India there was a much wider variety and Margaret found it hard to summon up much interest in them. Bertha explained that, having no car, she went shopping most days for what she required. Margaret was horrified. In Darjeeling her mother rarely went shopping – she chose what she wanted to order and one or more of the servants went and collected it. The prospect of having to shop daily when she was married was not a pleasant one to Margaret. In addition, she would have to carry the shopping home by hand – an even worse prospect.

The more she heard about the British way of life, the more she felt apprehensive about the future. Staring out of the windows onto the street across the road did not cheer her up; most of the time the weather was dull and damp, there was a clamminess to it that she was not used to. Despite the cast-iron radiators, she still felt cold and longed for the warmth and colour of India, and even for the warmth of the SS *Ragnera*. She also missed the debonair and kindly Ben, although Bertha and Walter had both done their best to make her feel welcome, and Margaret felt their friendliness and affection were genuine. After lunch she was in the lounge when the phone rang, and Bertha called her to come, as it was Ben on the phone.

Ben had obtained particulars of three available properties in the Beckenham area, and he offered to come over the following morning so they could view them together. Hearing Ben's familiar voice on the phone cheered Margaret up considerably, and for the rest of the day she felt very much more at peace and her mind was less disturbed.

Chapter 11

Finding a Home, and Meeting the Brethren

The next morning, Margaret was waiting for Ben when Clarkson pulled up in the Rolls in front of the house. She leapt to her feet, surprised to find how comforted she felt on seeing Ben again. With her father behind in Darjeeling, Ben had become like a father or uncle to her. Having lived a varied and successful life and travelled to many countries had allowed Ben to acquire a wide and practical knowledge of many aspects of life and he was considered 'worldly wise'. He came in to speak to Bertha about the three possible properties he had found that might be suitable for Edwyn and Margaret to rent. He fully understood that they would want to stay in the Beckenham area to be close to both Walter and Bertha and also Hubert. Margaret had met Hubert only briefly when he had called in the night before after work and Bertha had given him supper. Hubert had not been as fortunate as Edwyn in finding work, and currently was working as a deliveryman for a company who distributed their kitchen products to shops in the London area. He was not at all well informed about local property to rent, as he and Edwyn had found their small, top floor flat about five years previously and had lived in it together ever since.

Beckenham was not as fashionable a town as neighbouring Bickley or Chislehurst, but it had developed a lot over the previous fifty years due to the demand for homes close to London. The problem was to find a home affordable on Edwyn's salary. From what Margaret had told Ben about

Edwyn, he had deduced that he was the type of man who was likely to remain in the same job for years; it seemed to Ben that Edwyn was not a high flier or motivated to better himself, he was content to have a salary that provided just enough to live on and no more. Ben showed Margaret and Bertha the details of several places he had found, and Margaret became rather confused. As they looked at the descriptions, Ben explained why the rent varied depending on whether they were in a better area of the town or a less pleasant one. Proximity to the railway station also played a part in what the rent cost. Margaret understood this but choosing a place to live was becoming more complex than she had bargained for and she was thankful that Ben would go with her.

Before they left, Bertha had something she wanted to say to Margaret. 'You'll be wanting a family, no doubt, so I would suggest you choose a flat in a less favourable area and on the ground floor, so you will have some space and not be cramped. It's no fun in a poky flat.'

And, still feeling rather overawed by meeting Ben, and looking at his magnificent Rolls Royce, she spoke somewhat diffidently to him: 'And to think you have a chauffeur in uniform!'

Ben smiled at her, and Margaret smiled, as having been driven in the Rolls from Tilbury she had no qualms about getting into it again, and she had a feeling of security and comfort as she did so. Ben had found a map of the town and instructed Clarkson to drive to the first address; it was a second-floor flat in a pleasing area, there were parks and green spaces surrounding it, the houses were nicely spaced out and the shops were just at the end of the road. The agent was there to show them around and, although the flat was not large, Margaret fell in love with it, as she liked its location and the way the rooms had been decorated. However, Ben convinced her that a flat on the second floor with no lift would not be suitable if she and Edwyn were to have children. Arriving at the second flat, they found the agent again waiting for them. This flat was much larger, the rooms were a good size and it was on the ground floor. But the flat was not in a good state – wallpaper was peeling off the walls and the carpets were nearly threadbare. As she looked at the rooms, Margaret expressed her distaste. 'This quite upsets me,' she told Ben. 'I could not live in a place like this; it has not been cared for at all.'

Ben agreed; he could see that she had a refined nature and said: 'We must see what the next place offers. In fact, it is a very small house in a different area of Beckenham.' As they drove through the centre of town, Margaret stared at the roads they passed and at the shops; she looked in vain for anything to remind her of home in Darjeeling, but there was nothing. The Rolls stopped outside a row of small Victorian, terraced houses in a long road called Beckenham Grove. Ben was encouraged. 'This looks a bit better,' he said.

And Margaret, still feeling she was a stranger in this new country, was not greatly heartened but she had to agree. The agent showed them round the house. It was very small indeed but had two bedrooms and a separate lounge with a small dining area, plus a kitchen and bathroom. The rent was less than the first flat in the more salubrious area, but shops were nearby and a pleasant park was not too far away. Margaret looked around the house – she felt it to be extremely cramped and confining, but it was not badly decorated and an improvement on the previous two flats they had seen.

'Ben,' she said, 'of the three we've seen, I feel this is the best one. At least there is an upstairs.'

And Ben agreed. The rent was just within the amount Edwyn had specified, and he informed the agent that Margaret would take it. Fortuitously, the agent was amenable to keeping the house available to her until Edwyn arrived.

After taking Margaret back to Bertha, Ben left, telling Margaret to phone him for anything else she needed help with. Margaret looked around her at Bertha's house and wondered how she would cope looking after a house – she had no knowledge of how to run a home. Housework, cooking, ironing and shopping were unknown to her – in India there were always the 'boys' to do all of these. If the husband was not earning a huge salary it did not matter since labour was incredibly cheap, and the Anglo-Indians did no practical work at all. She tried to push all this out of her mind and not dwell on it.

The next few weeks flew by. Margaret needed to find a church where they could be married but she had no idea how to do this and Bertha and Walter were not much help since they were not churchgoers. Hubert was out at work all day apart from the weekends, but he too knew nothing about churches or arranging marriages. But Ben was there to help Margaret in every way. He finalised the rent agreement for the small Victorian house and took her to see the nearest Anglican church. Margaret, who had been brought up as a Catholic, had some doubts. 'I don't consider myself a member of the Catholic church now; in fact, I find it hard to believe in any faith. Would this be a blockage to getting married in an Anglican church, as Edwyn would want?'

'I'm sure there will be no problem,' Ben reassured her. 'Vicars are becoming liberal now.'

He took her to meet the vicar of their nearest Anglican church, a kindly, calm and unhurried man. Margaret liked him, but remorse kicked in once again, as she felt she was approaching him deceitfully since she was not a virgin. Of course, she could not tell him this, neither did she tell Ben. The vicar saw no problem to the marriage and was happy to agree an approximate date with them. Edwyn had told Margaret to choose a date that was soon after his return from Bombay – he was anxious for them to be married and living together. Now she had found the church, there was no more for Margaret to do and there was over a month to go before Edwyn was due to return. The weeks were going by, and Margaret found herself feeling a little less strange in the country, although she became rather apprehensive as Edwyn's arrival came nearer.

She had almost forgotten that Dr Crofton had promised to get in touch with her when he returned to England for his two months' leave. However, he had not forgotten his promise and once back he went to visit her. She was surprised how affected she was to see him again, and so pleased that he had kept his word. She remembered how kind and discreet he had been when she was pregnant, and how he had taken her to his house for a few days to allow her to recover after she had given baby Grace away. When they met, the good doctor was gratified to see she was adjusting to British culture. The first thing he did was to drive her over to Worthing to introduce her to his daughter, Joyce, with whom he was staying. Joyce had already been in touch with Margaret by phone several times, and Margaret was looking forward to meeting her since they were of a similar age. Amazingly, they took to each other immediately. Dr Crofton never once mentioned a word about baby Grace to his daughter, and he was quietly content when he saw how well the two of them got on. Joyce begged him to invite Margaret to stay with them for the following weekend, and he did.

The following Saturday, when she arrived at Worthing station, they explained that they would be going to the Brethren meeting on the Sunday morning, and Margaret, feeling so much at home with them both, said she would come with them. To her surprise, the Meeting was conducted in a very different way to the Catholic service she had been used to in India, and she liked the simple, unfussy way in which it took place. After the Meeting people stayed on for a cup of tea and a chat and Margaret noticed they all seemed genuinely interested in each other's lives. Joyce introduced her to John Templeford and Janice Simpson, a young couple about to get married. Janice was delighted to meet Margaret and loved hearing about her life in India and wanted to hear more. She was a lively young woman with a personality that attracted people to her.

'Why Margaret,' she said, 'It's going to be another month before your fiancé gets home. You must be getting a bit fed up living in someone else's house. Why not come down and spend a few days with me and my family? John is a doctor and works all day and some weekends in Littlehampton, but I'd love to see you, and we must keep in touch after we are both married.'

'I'd like that very much,' replied Margaret, thinking what an attractive person Janice was. 'I could come next week.'

'Yes, do come on Monday and stay until Friday; I will meet your train.'

And so Margaret met Janice's parents and spent four days with them. The two young women very quickly formed a lasting friendship. On the Wednesday evening, Janice took Margaret to the Brethren mid-week Bible Study meeting and she felt totally at ease there; the group welcomed her without her feeling they were trying to convert her. Dr Crofton and Joyce were both there, and for the first time since she had arrived in England Margaret felt she was among true friends. On the Friday she travelled back by train to Edwyn's aunt and as she left her two new friends, Janice and Joyce, she felt quite bereft, but Dr Crofton promised that he knew a young woman in London he could introduce her to.

He was true to his word, and the following week he contacted the Collins family in Guildford. Arnold and Ingrid Collins – she was Swedish – were a recently married young couple, also members of the Plymouth Brethren. They invited Margaret over for the following weekend and, as she had done with Joyce, on the Sunday they all went to the local Brethren meeting in Guildford. Although the Meeting was full of strangers, Margaret had the same feeling she had had in Worthing, that these were kind and genuine people. Ingrid was also someone Margaret felt drawn too. Although she was not as outgoing as Janice, Margaret felt there was a sense of calm about her.

Margaret took away a sense of sincerity with her and wished she had been going to get married in the Brethren meeting rather than the Anglican church but felt sure Edwyn would not agree to this. She had told him about being brought up as a Catholic and Edwyn had said he would not be happy to be married in a Catholic church, and as this meant little to her now she had agreed with him. Having met Dr Crofton, Joyce and the two young Brethren ladies, Margaret was uncertain as to what she believed, yet at the same time she was very drawn to the Brethren way of faith but doubted that Edwyn would encourage this.

The Brethren belief originated in Dublin in the 1820s, and adhered to a low church, evangelical faith, with the Bible being the supreme authority for church doctrine. There was a conviction that adult or nearly adult baptism was the right way, as this allowed the person to be sufficiently mature to have made their own committed declaration of faith. Instead of churches, they had Assemblies, and the Open Brethren were happy to link themselves to their local Anglican churches. The Closed Brethren, however, believed that they should have a 'separation from the world', and this could even go as far as not allowing their children to mix with their neighbour's children if the neighbours did not share their belief. Since Margaret had put her Catholic faith on hold, she took on the atmosphere of the Assemblies rather than their doctrine.

Meanwhile in Bombay, Edwyn was counting the days until he returned to England; he wrote to Margaret frequently and even managed to get through on the phone from time to time. Looking forward to a calm and happy marriage to Margaret, he envisioned living in a simple, modest home with few extravagances. Not motivated by any aspirations of wealth and luxury, he was content with his present fairly lowly job and had no wish to better it; his desire for the future was only that his uncomplicated life would remain so.

By the time he arrived at Tilbury, also by ship, he was impatient to get to London and then to Beckenham. He thought that Margaret might get lost in central London if she came to meet him there, so he had told her he would phone her when he knew what time his train was arriving in Beckenham, and she was to wait for him at his aunt and uncle's home. Madly in love with her as he was, he already knew she was not of a realistic and down-to-earth nature, and he was perfectly prepared to see to the practical side of matters when they were married. Arriving finally at the house in Beckenham Grove, he found Margaret sitting in the hall waiting for him. Overjoyed to see her at last, he held her close and could not stop kissing her. She was a trifle overcome by such strong emotions and found she was rather hesitant in responding to him. The past eighteen months had taken their toll on her, and now that Edwyn was home she found herself hesitant to take the final step of committing herself for life to a marriage.

'What would I have done without Ben's help? I am here in England now, a continent away from my respectable Catholic family in India and I may never see my parents or my brothers again. I hope I'm doing the right thing by marrying Edwyn, but I don't see how I can get out of it now,' she thought.

Then she reminded herself that by marrying Edwyn she was able to leave behind all her past troubles and misfortunes in India and start a new life here in England.

'It must be right,' she told herself. 'Edwyn is stable, solid and decent; I'll be safe with him and this is what I need.'

But a small shiver of doubt disturbed her as she watched Bertha work steadily at maintaining the house and garden.

'She does nothing else but housework, shopping, cooking and ironing, and when that is done she starts on the garden. She hardly goes out socially at all; it's not much of a life,' she thought.

She sat with Edwyn in the lounge, going over the plans they had made for their wedding. It was arranged for early July 1928 and now that Edwyn was here the banns could be read. Edwyn would continue to work for the Civil Service in London, travelling up by train every weekday, and they would live in the cramped little house in Beckenham until they could afford something better.

Margaret made her own simple wedding dress from a roll of cream satin material she'd found in a local shop – she had always been able to sew, as this was one thing her mother had taught her. It was not the heavy satin that was worn on special occasions by the wealthy Indians, but of a lesser quality; nevertheless, the dress looked charming on her.

And so they were married quietly at St Barnabas' church. Walter, Bertha and Hubert came, as did Dr Crofton, Joyce, John and Janice Templeford and Arnold and Ingrid Collins. Her new life had really begun.

CHAPTER 12

Ten Years Married, and Pregnancy

Now that she was respectably married, Margaret wrote to her parents quite often. She tried to make the letters cheerful so that she could assure them she was doing well. George and Martha Horton were delighted each time a letter arrived; most of their sons had departed to countries such as America and Australia and to other parts of India. Once the brothers had Margaret's address in England, some of them wrote to her and she was glad of the contact. Leonard, a devout Catholic, wrote regularly to her, assuring her of his prayers.

However, in reality Margaret was downhearted. 'How could nearly ten years have gone by? And yet they have dragged,' she thought, as she struggled to carry the shopping into the small kitchen. She noticed the floor needed cleaning and so did the work surfaces. The living room too had not been cleaned for a week, let alone the bedrooms upstairs.

'And now I must think what to have for dinner tonight. What a bore, it seems one meal after another these days. What with shopping, cleaning, preparing meals, laying tables, washing up and ironing there is nothing in my life I find worthwhile. By the time Edwyn comes home I am dead tired; he tells me about his day and I don't know why but I cannot summon up any interest in it.'

Pursing her lips, she thought back ruefully to when she had met Jane Cullington; it seemed so long ago and now she seldom saw her. It was before she had married Edwyn. Lord and Lady Cullingon were friends of Ben's in London, and one weekend Ben was invited to a luncheon party they were giving. The Cullingtons were a well-to-do couple and when they entertained Jane always asked Ben if he would like to bring anyone with him. He usually said no but knowing that Margaret's life was likely to be mundane and lacking in interest and stimulation he thought she would benefit from meeting the Cullingtons. Jane had always loved Indian saris and materials and wanted to go to India and so she immediately said yes.

'Perhaps you could introduce her to some of your friends?' said Ben. 'She is a lovely young lady, but she is still adapting to our culture and is understandably a little out of her depth here. I am sure both you and your friends will love meeting her.'

'Of course,' replied Jane, a cheerful, friendly lady in her early fifties. 'Bring her over with you this Sunday; we are having a small luncheon party and you will both be welcome to join us.'

Wearing her best dress, Margaret had gone with Ben to the lunch. She found a delightfully furnished home adorned with mementoes and valuable ornaments; embossed wallpaper decorated the rooms and the Regency furniture appealed to Margaret; from her comments, it was obvious to the others there that she appreciated beauty and had good taste. There were two other older couples there as guests and at first Margaret was a little unforthcoming, but Ben and Jane brought her out, and she found everyone there loved hearing about her life in India. Jane Cullington was absolutely entranced by Margaret; she had no children of her own and she recognised in Margaret a warm nature and a certain ladylikeness. From that moment on she invited Margaret to a number of her lunches and dinners and showed her around London, where they visited several of the museums and art galleries. Margaret was absolutely in her element and she and Jane became almost like mother and daughter.

Margaret, now standing by the kitchen table with the shopping, was contemplating the chores she must do before Edwyn got home. Yet she seemed almost unable to get going with these jobs. Since her marriage, Margaret had not been able to see as much of Jane as she would have liked. Jane had been in contact with her frequently, inviting her to lunches and outings, but Margaret had become almost moribund in her small house in Beckenham. Despite Jane's invitations, she seldom went up to London for the day, but this afternoon she realised that she had not seen Jane for over six months and she felt desperate to see her again. She rushed around the house, cleaning the kitchen and the bedroom, and preparing their meal. She had fifteen minutes before Edwyn got home, and so she phoned Jane and arranged a time to meet for lunch the following Wednesday.

She recalled that when she had first met Jane, ten years earlier, before her marriage to Edwyn, she had spoken enthusiastically about her to Walter, Bertha and Hubert, but they had not responded with much interest; they tended to consider people like the Cullingtons rather affected and pretentious and not relevant to their daily life. But for Margaret the way the Cullingtons lived their lives attracted her; it was not just that they lived well but they were charitable too. Ralph Cullington was the president of a society that raised money for families who were living on very little or no income – some did not even have enough to clothe and feed their children. And Jane Cullington supported a charity helping disabled children. Margaret had liked this about them – they were wealthy but they did not flaunt their wealth, and they were aware of the needs of those less fortunate. The more Margaret had seen of Jane and Ralph, the more she had felt comfortable with their friends and their way of life.

'I would like to be like that,' she had thought. 'Live well with lovely things around me and be generous to those with less money. But this is not going to happen when I'm married to Edwyn, as I know he is going to be content with a basic salary and I doubt if he will want to forge ahead. I have no money of my own, so I must be satisfied with what I will have, although this will not be much.'

She was right, and nearly ten years later she was in the same situation, having to do all the domestic chores with no money for little luxuries, such as trips to London or delicious meals in good restaurants as she had enjoyed with Jane. Since she had been married to Edwyn she had had to cut down her outings with Jane, as Edwyn thought Jane was of a 'la-de-dah' class and was not happy for Margaret to mix with her. Jane had just laughed and told Margaret to take no notice of him, but Margaret knew that Edwyn was serious and she did not want to risk upsetting him. The reality was that Edwyn had been brought up not to expect too much in life, and to be content with an adequate but fairly lowly income. Both his father and mother had lived like this, his two brothers also, and it did not enter his head to strive for more.

Margaret was different. Her upbringing in a white family in Darjeeling had accustomed her to a certain way of living. A life where women were not called upon to be domesticated, merely to be the administrators of household tasks, just to give the orders to the servants who then carried out the work. Living in England, Margaret had been shocked to find that married women spent their day doing household chores; her time in Darjeeling had taught her nothing about coping with these – married women there were free to socialise with their friends at the various clubs. Jane was sympathetic but could not advise her much as she herself employed staff. Margaret could now only escape from what she called 'drudgery' about once a month to meet with Jane and be taken out for a meal or a visit to one of London's sites or art galleries, but now it was six months since she had seen her. On top of this the fog, the cold and the wet and damp winters did not help; on Edwyn's salary they could only afford to heat their bedroom and the living room; the hall, the kitchen and the bathroom were all unheated, something Margaret would never become accustomed to. Trying to cook in a cold kitchen in winter took it out of her, and there were times when she was in tears.

When she met Jane the following week, she complained: 'I am so terribly done in by all the domestic tasks I have to do. I have no energy left by the evening when Edwyn gets home.'

'You have not married the right man,' Jane replied. 'Edwyn is going nowhere; he is likely to stay at the same low level in the Civil Service for the rest of his working life.'

Hearing this Margaret felt even more depressed; her future seemed bleak. Furthermore, she was worried as she had been unable to get pregnant in the nine years since she had married Edwyn, despite consulting various doctors over the years.

'I've been trying to get pregnant and time is going on; I'm thirty-five now,' she said. 'Last week I saw a gynaecologist and I have to have a small operation next week to turn my womb.'

'How on earth could your womb have got out of place?' queried Jane.

Margaret, about to tell her that it must have been when she gave birth to Grace, controlled herself in time to say: 'I don't know, and I'm hoping that after this operation I will become pregnant.'

Jane sympathised with what Margaret said, as she herself had been unable to have children, and not knowing anything about Margaret's past she felt compassion for her. If Margaret had only been able to have a baby

Jane would have loved to have been a godmother and given her godchild presents and taken her or him on outings.

The following week Margaret had the operation and was told to wait a month before trying again to get pregnant but was reassured that her womb was now positioned correctly and she could expect to have a child. Edwyn was patient with all this; he took things as they occurred. Despite his wish for a child, he was phlegmatic about it – if it did not happen he would accept it.

Four months after having the operation Margaret suspected she might be pregnant. She delayed two more weeks before going to the doctor, but then to her immense joy he confirmed the pregnancy. Margaret could hardly speak with excitement. When Edwyn came home that night she told him the news and he too was pleased, not the extreme pleasure that Margaret felt but nevertheless he had a good feeling about becoming a father.

'I can see how happy you are,' he said to Margaret.

'I can't believe that at last I'm expecting a baby. I've waited years for this,' she replied. 'I will have my very own baby to love and nurture, and I will keep her close to me for always.'

Edwyn laughed. 'He or she will grow up you know, and maybe leave home and get married.'

'Even if she does get married I hope she will never live far away from me,' said Margaret.

'How do you know the baby will be a girl?' queried Edwyn.

Margaret was adamant in her conviction that this child would replace the baby she had lost and replied: 'I feel sure it will be.'

Having lost her beloved Grace, Margaret made no bones about admitting she wanted a girl, but of course she did not tell anyone why this was. She had kept in touch with Joyce, Janice and Ingrid by phone and letter, but had hardly seen them since her marriage. On one brief occasion the four of them had met in London for lunch at Lyons Corner House by Charing Cross station. These three Brethren Christian friends meant so much to Margaret and the friendships were to last a lifetime. Due to her continuing contact with Janice and Ingrid, plus the friendship of Dr Crofton and Joyce, Margaret had from time to time managed to get to her local Brethren afternoon women's meetings, where she was warmly welcomed and felt at home.

With the prospect of a baby that would be her very own, Margaret's frame of mind lifted and even though she felt a bit sick at first, she never complained. The months passed happily for both of them and then the day came when Margaret recognised that labour was starting. It was a Saturday evening and Edwyn took her at once to the nursing home and then went to the waiting room. Before long, a nurse came and told him to go home, as the baby would not be born for several hours.

Margaret had experienced the pains of labour before, so she had time to take in her surroundings – a plainly furnished, single room. Two nurses had been in to see her, both of them kind and efficient, and they had assumed that it was her first birth and she did not tell them otherwise. As the night progressed, the pains became ever more severe and the pain relief offered was not much help.

However, at four-thirty the following morning, on 7 July, 1938, the doctor was called to deliver the baby and Margaret's long-awaited child was born – it was a perfect little girl. She heard the doctor saying this, and her joy knew no bounds. At last, her very own child and this time one she could keep for ever. As Margaret held her baby for the first time, tears ran down her face. Edwyn came in very soon after to see them both and he too was delighted with his daughter and quietly content when he saw that Margaret was so happy.

Several days later Edwyn collected Margaret and the baby from the nursing home and took them home. They had previously discussed names – if it had been a boy Margaret wanted to call him Christopher and if it was a girl Patricia.

'I would like to call her Patricia,' she told Edwyn, once they were home, and Edwyn was perfectly content to do this.

Baby Patricia was no trouble; Margaret doted on her and vowed she would never tell her about her past in Darjeeling but would give Patricia the best life she could. She wanted her to have a life like the Cullingtons – a lovely home, beautiful things around her and enough money to enjoy the many pleasures of London, maybe even of France and other European countries. Margaret had never forgotten the short time she had spent in France on the way to England from Bombay – the delicious food, the culture and the ambience had made their mark on her for life.

Chapter 13

Leamington Spa, and the War

After Patricia was born, Margaret managed to persuade Edwyn that she needed someone to clean the house once a week – with a baby to look after she just could not cope with everything. So Mrs McKenna came weekly, a stout, robust woman who was a natural in all practical matters. Seeing that Margaret was somewhat inept in the home, she would not only clean the house on her weekly visits but would also prepare some meals to put in the fridge for a couple of days. Margaret did not tell Edwyn about the cooking she did and he did not ask.

'Mrs McKenna, you are amazing,' Margaret told her. 'You work so fast and so thoroughly and having a couple of meals that I just need to reheat is such a help to me.'

'Don't worry, love,' said the capable woman, 'I like coming here and seeing you and the baby; I'm fond of you both and I can see you are struggling.'

Indeed, she was; an upbringing in Darjeeling had laid the foundation of a distinctive way of life for Margaret, a life free of domestic duties. Being naturally warm-hearted and outgoing, she had always been popular and her life had moved along smoothly and easily until she met Gordon McCall. Even now, years later, she recalled this affair with resentment, and bitter feelings gnawed into her yet again.

One evening, when Patricia was about eighteen months, Edwyn came home and told Margaret that there were rumours of war with Germany.

'What would this mean for us?' Margaret asked him.

'If we do go to war with Germany I've been told that I will need to stay in my job here in London and do what's necessary to help our country. But if this happens I don't want you and Patricia to stay anywhere near London.'

Talk of war terrified Margaret, and she knew enough to realise that London would be a target for any bombs.

'What could Patricia and I do?' she said.

'I'm not sure yet, but I would like you to be evacuated to somewhere safer than London.'

A few weeks later Edwyn was certain that the country was going to war with Germany. He spoke to Ben, as he guessed he would want to be away from London too. Ben had already made his plans to rent a large house in Leamington Spa, a town he felt would be much safer than London. He knew how worried Edwyn was about Margaret and Patricia, and willingly offered to have them both live with him for as long as the war lasted. Edwyn was mightily relieved to feel his wife and child could be placed in a safer area of the country.

And so, in September 1940, Margaret and Patricia were sent down to Leamington Spa to live with Ben and Margaret now found herself staying in a large house with many rooms. A cook and a 'daily' help looked after Ben's needs, much to Margaret's relief. Cook did the shopping and cooked the meals for everyone, while the 'daily' went through the house methodically throughout the week seeing it was kept clean. This arrangement suited Margaret perfectly, and she helped Ben by directing Cook and discussing with her what they would eat. Of course, rationing was in operation and foodstuffs such as meat, eggs and butter were very scarce, so recipes involving carrots were predominant! However, extra foodstuffs did come into the house, as Ben had a way of finding 'black market' food, and so they lived well throughout the war. Edwyn was sending Margaret money but was unaware that Ben was more than doubling this in providing better-quality food for Margaret and Patricia.

There was little enemy action in Leamington Spa and almost no bombing, but the windows had to be covered at night with blackout curtains so that the indoor lights would not show. Whenever the air raid warning sounded, which was infrequently, Margaret would bundle

Patricia into her green siren suit and get her quickly down to the basement, which had been made into a shelter for times like this. Blankets were put down to make it comfortable to spend the night there. Patricia thought it was rather fun, but Margaret was more aware of the danger and always imagined them being bombed. Indeed, the worst-hit nearby town was Coventry, where the cathedral was bombed and destroyed in November 1941 and many lives were lost. Overall, Ben's choice of a town to live in during the years of war proved to be a sound one. A doctor and his wife, the Reynolds, lived quietly next door; they had no children and Patricia often found her way into their garden and climbed up the steps leading to the front door to talk to the wife. Margaret was not too happy about this, assuming she was bothering Mrs Reynolds, and she would usually go round and fetch her back.

'Mrs Reynolds is not used to children,' she told Patricia. 'If you go there, you must not stay long, no more than fifteen minutes.'

'But she likes talking to me,' argued Patricia. 'And last time she invited me into her house, and do you know something, she has two pet rabbits just outside her kitchen and one of them, Dorcas, is expecting a baby in two weeks. She asked me if I would like to come and see the baby rabbit when it is born.'

Margaret had always been hesitant about being a burden to other people; she was conscious of Ben's generosity is housing Patricia and herself, and she was strict about making sure that Patricia did not bother him, but when she heard about the rabbits she relented and said: 'If Mrs Reynolds invited you, then that's all right, Patricia, you can go.'

Two weeks went by, Patricia counting the days, and when the date arrived she dashed round to the Reynoldss after school. Sadly, the rabbit had not yet been born but Patricia was impatient to see the baby. Mrs Reynolds promised to let her know as soon as the rabbit arrived, and two days later she knocked on the door to say: 'Dorcas gave birth last night and she has had five babies! You can come round to see them now.'

Patricia was so excited and visited the rabbits every day to see how they had grown. After eight weeks, four of them were sold and Patricia begged Margaret for the fifth one, a female. Ben was asked and said they could buy a hutch for the one rabbit, but it must live either alone or with another female. And so, the baby rabbit arrived and lived at the bottom of the garden with another female that Margaret bought. She thought about her own childhood and the animals that were often near their house – it seemed natural to find them around. They were not always identifiable, but deer, small bears, fruit bats, shrews and lizards were common and some of them even found their way into the house; in India this was not uncommon.

Margaret thought to herself: 'How different our life is at the moment, Ben sees we lack for nothing. Life is not going to be the same at all once the war ends.'

But the war went on for five years. Edwyn visited them only infrequently, as the train service during the war years was intermittent. When he came, he could not help noticing how well Ben was living – the big house, a live-in cook and no lack of butter, vegetables, eggs and meat. Although he was pleased to see his wife and child looked after so well, he was not so pleased to see how Ben's standard of living was so much above his own.

Patricia went to a little private school nearby, which Ben paid for; he knew enough about Margaret's background in India to recognise that she placed great store on a good education for Patricia. Patricia loved her school and the teacher told Margaret how well she was doing. Being an only child, she was content to amuse herself. At meals Margaret would tell Ben about the small things that made up her day and assure him that the household arrangements were taken care of. Now in his early seventies, Ben loved having the younger woman with him in the house – she brought a warmth to the place that he had not experienced since his wife had died.

Chapter 14

Back to Domesticity

In September 1945 the war ended, but in the UK its effect was felt for some years afterwards. The country's finances were at a low ebb, caused in part by its debt to the USA, the Anglo-American loan, made primarily to support British overseas expenditure in the immediate post-war years. Food was not plentiful and rationing continued for another nine years until 1954. Immigrants needed to be brought in to meet the need caused by labour shortages. They came from the Caribbean, the West Indies, from Africa and, of course, from some of the European countries. Although they were needed, they were not all welcomed, and some of the British turned against them and started fights and riots. Despite all of this, after the dreary years of war, people wanted some glamour, and so fashion and the arts flourished.

Margaret and Patricia returned to London. Ben sold his house in Wilbraham Place in 1945 and bought a pleasant house in Bromley, Kent. He had sold his wine and spirit business before the war, and now bought three small properties in the London suburbs, which he rented out. Edwyn and Margaret bought a house in a nearby road; it was not as imposing as Ben's but was adequate for the three of them. Patricia was now seven and went to Mount Crescent School, essentially a private preparatory school for girls going on later to public school. Ben had offered to pay the school fees. Margaret was once again responsible for all the household tasks and after living with Ben at no cost for five years and having staff to manage the house, she did not take to these easily. The stone floor in the hall was cold and hard to keep clean, the rugs in the lounge kept getting rucked up, and the upstairs bedrooms seemed endless to clean and never seemed to be warm. After the comfort of the lovely home in Leamington Spa, which the staff kept spotless, she was conscious of struggling to keep her present home even moderately clean and tidy; let alone coping with the shopping, cooking and ironing, plus looking after Patricia. In truth, looking after Patricia was what she wanted to spend her time doing. Patricia was now at school full time, and when she came home mid-afternoon Margaret simply wanted to be with her, talk to her about her day and build a close relationship with her. But she often found she had not got around to preparing the evening meal or cleaning the kitchen and, having to do these, she frequently had to leave Patricia to her own devices. Repeatedly, she looked back at her own childhood – despite her brothers going off with each other, there had always been someone around for company, but Patricia was an only child and Margaret worried about this. So, however exhausted she felt or whatever else she had to do she would always say to Patricia: 'I know you like to have time with your friends after school, and you can bring one of them back to tea anytime you like. Not all together though, just one at a time!'

'Oh, Mummy, thank you, thank you. I have lots of friends, and three of them are like me, they don't have brothers or sisters.'

So Diana, Jean and Ruth were all invited back to tea again and again after school; Margaret made them sandwiches and small sponge cakes and although this tired her afterwards, Patricia's pleasure was its own reward. Her great fear was that some accident or medical problem might happen to her beloved daughter, and she watched over her persistently, scrutinising her for any sign of ill health and making sure she was safe at all times.

'Mummy, don't fuss over me,' Patricia said.

'You are so precious to me, darling, I can't risk anything happening to you. I want the very best for you, I want you to have a happy life and when you are grown up I want you to marry someone wealthy so that you don't have to spend your life toiling at domestic chores.'

'I don't think I will like domestic chores, and I don't like seeing you having to work, work, work. When we lived with Uncle Ben we did what we wanted and he had people to do all this.'

Margaret was touched at the child's understanding, and replied: 'Yes, he did, and due to his generosity we had a good life with him throughout the war years. But now we're back to living with Daddy and we have much less money and there is little that we can afford. Which is why I want you to have a better life.'

No more was said by either of them, but Patricia did not fully understand why they were not still living with Ben and having an easier life.

Margaret was trying her best to become accustomed to living with Edwyn again, but his low income meant there was little money left over for any treats or small luxuries. Edwyn was perfectly content to live without these since he considered them a waste of money. Occasionally, Ben, seeing how Margaret was pushed to make ends meet, would come round with a chicken, a ham or some butter. Where he obtained these Margaret never knew, but she was grateful for anything he brought. Edwyn, however, was not at all pleased by Ben's generosity and in fact he discouraged it. He knew he owed Ben a debt for looking after Margaret and Patricia during the long war years, yet something in him held back from making a friend of the older man. Ben was always affable towards him, but Edwyn disliked him. He knew that Margaret and Patricia had become accustomed to a much higher standard of living and he resented this immensely.

Margaret tried desperately to cope, not only with the low income but with living with a man who had no ambition and was clearly going to stay at the bottom of the ladder financially. When Edwyn went off to the office each weekday and Patricia had gone to school, she would often go up to the bedroom and cry: she cried for the frustration of her present life and she cried for the thought of the future which held no change for the better. She looked at how Ben was living and how he had a live-in cook and a woman who came to clean three times a week, and she compared her life with his. One afternoon in August 1946, when Ben arrived with a leg of lamb and some butter for her, she could not help saying: 'Why am I so miserable, Ben? I should be happier. We are not on the breadline but compared with my upbringing in Darjeeling and especially the time we lived with you during the war my life now feels barren and hopeless. The thought that this will go on without improvement fills me with dread.'

'I know how hard you are finding life now, Margaret,' replied Ben. 'It's a complete change for you, and the lack of money means you have little help. I can see too that you're not domestically minded, it's just not in your nature.'

'That's true, I'm not gifted that way. I see other women really enjoying all these jobs, and I wonder why I don't. My neighbour spends her day cooking, cleaning, ironing and shopping, and she loves it. She has no wish to do anything else.'

'You are not like that, though,' said Ben. 'You are made for better things, my dear. I wish I could give you a more leisurely life, one where you could live in a lovely home and have staff to run the place. One where you could have trips to London to go shopping, go to the theatre and meet your friends.'

At that moment Margaret looked at Ben and saw that he truly did mean what he said. He was looking at her in a manner that she had not noticed before, it was a manner that said, 'If you were mine I would give you all these things.'

'He really does care about me,' she thought. 'And he understands me.'

She looked at him and a look passed between them that changed the way they related to each other for ever. Margaret just said: 'Yes, I would like that immensely.'

And Ben replied: 'Then it must happen.'

No more was said, but from that moment Margaret knew she could not go on living with Edwyn.

Chapter 15

Dorothy, A Second Marriage, and a New Rolls Royce

She thought of Patricia and how she wanted the best life for her, and she knew this would not happen while she and Edwyn were still married. Never before had she thought about marrying Ben – he had always been the kindly, understanding uncle to her. But now she could have a relationship with him that would mean total security and a comfortable life for her and Patricia. Patricia would be able to go to private schools, maybe even be presented to the Queen – Ben moved in such circles. Her imagination took off and she felt she could now look forward to a better life.

From then on, Ben and Margaret never spoke openly about it, but the agreement was obvious to them both and eventually Ben guided Margaret in the process of divorce.

However, a few weeks previously, in July 1946, Ben had recently had an unexpected shock. Twenty-five years before he had stayed in Edinburgh while on a touring holiday in Scotland. One evening he dined at a restaurant near his hotel and, knowing about good wines and spirits, had ordered a particularly good wine. He asked for a half bottle but was told by the waitress that they did not have half bottles of that particular wine and so he settled for a bottle. Having eaten a very leisurely dinner and drunk most of the wine, he signalled to the waitress and asked for the bill.

The Raj, the Rolls, and the Remorse

By this time Ben was the last person in the restaurant, and even the restaurant owner had gone home. The waitress appeared with the bill: 'Here we are, Sir, I hope that is right?'

Ben checked the bill, found it to be correct and paid it. He looked up to find the waitress looking at him in a slightly inviting manner, and suddenly he saw her in a new light, as a likeable and attractive woman of about thirty-five. Totally out of character, Ben was immediately smitten by her and asked her if she would like to go for a drink. She smilingly acquiesced and Ben took her to a bar that he knew stayed open late. They talked and talked and got on well – so well that Ben invited her to spend the night with him at his hotel. This was completely out of character for Ben, and he later blamed all the wine he'd drunk.

The following morning the woman had left before Ben woke up, but not before she had noted down his address and phone number from the hotel register. Ben woke to find her gone and wondered what on earth had possessed him to sleep with a woman he barely knew. As she had left, he assumed that she had not wished to see him again in the morning and had sensibly slipped away before he woke. He cursed himself throughout the morning for what had happened, and then tried to shrug it off and continued his touring holiday. Back home in London, in his apartment in Wilbraham Place, he forgot all about it. That was, until three months later when, while he was listening at home one evening to a Puccini opera, his phone rang.

'Hello, Ben speaking.'

'Good evening, Ben, this is Marilyn.'

Searching in his mind for who she might be, he replied: 'Um… just remind me where we met, Marylin.'

'Ben, we met in a restaurant in Edinburgh, and later at your hotel.'

Suddenly Ben was jolted out of his pleasant evening and remembered the whole thing.

'Oh… Marylin, how are you?' he said.

'I'm well, thank you, but I thought you should know that I'm expecting a baby.'

It took Ben a minute to fully grasp the situation. Surely the baby was someone else's but she was laying the blame on him, but before he could reply she continued: 'You are the father, I have proof of this. I want this baby and am going to have it, but I will need some support financially.'

Ben relaxed somewhat. If it was only money she wanted, that was not too much of a problem. They talked some more and Ben agreed to send Marylin a sum each month. She seemed satisfied with this and did not push him to acknowledge the baby; she was prepared to bring up the child herself. Ben was relieved to hear this since he had no wish to be further involved.

The arrangement had worked perfectly well for twenty-four years, until a few months before, in June 1946, when Marylin had unexpectedly died aged fifty-eight, leaving a will that cited Ben as her daughter's father. On Marilyn's death, her executor put her daughter, Dorothy, in touch with Ben.

Dorothy travelled down to London to meet Ben and she persuaded him to let her live with him. Since he was her father and had previously taken no part in her upbringing, he felt it was the least he could do now and saw no reason to object. However, after a few weeks it became apparent that Dorothy, now twenty-four, had grown into a rather unattractive woman and her character matched her looks. She was sullen and rude, lounged around all day smoking and, as a result, was not at all likeable and had no friends.

Ben confided this to Margaret, saying he had not yet told Dorothy that they were going to be married.

Ben cursed his one misdemeanour. Having Dorothy to live with him certainly cramped his style, and didn't find acceptance with his friends, but he explained to people that Dorothy was the daughter of an old friend of his who had died. He was desperate to get her married, but this was easier said than done, and there was no one on the horizon who was the least interested in Dorothy. This blow came just at the time when Ben and Margaret were hoping to get together. Ben entreated all his friends to find a man who might take Dorothy on; he even took her on a trip around Scotland and another extended trip around Africa in the hopes of meeting someone who would marry her, but nothing came of either of these trips.

Three months later a friend of Ben's introduced him to the Compton family. Their son, Richard Compton, had a deformed leg and a pronounced limp and due to this had become reticent and withdrawn, rarely taking part in social occasions. His mother, Mary, tried hard to get him to meet people but with little success. When Ben met the Compton family he saw the possibility of Richard and Dorothy getting together and invited the family over. Surprisingly, Richard fell for Dorothy, and Dorothy was persuaded that here was her chance to get married, but she was reluctant since Richard was unemployed. Ben needed to resolve this situation. He knew a contact in the United States who had recently written to him about his thriving steel business in San Diego, California, and he had mentioned that he was looking for someone to administer the sales side. Ben phoned him to enquire what skills were necessary for the post and was told that the new recruit needed only basic skills and could learn on the job. A couple of phone calls later and it was agreed that Richard Compton could have the position. Ben spoke to Richard: 'This job is now yours if you would like it. The salary is enough to keep both you and Dorothy in reasonable comfort, and San Diego has a warm and pleasant climate. Dorothy will like this, she has always wanted to live in the States.'

'This sounds very interesting,' replied Richard. 'If you're certain I could have this job, I would like to take it. It will be a relief to have guaranteed work and some money coming in.'

'Yes, the job is certain, I have it in writing,' said Ben.

'I'll take it then. Dorothy has agreed to marry me once I have work,' Richard replied.

Now the job was settled, Dorothy accepted Richard's proposal, and they were married before they set off for the States. To make sure they went, Ben paid for their passage, plus gave them some additional money to help them find somewhere to live. They departed and were never heard of again.

Ben was now free to marry Margaret, and it remained for her to find a way to leave Edwyn.

Before speaking to him, she thought a lot about what she would say to Edwyn but when she did she found he was not totally surprised. Edwyn was quite aware of problems in their marriage; he had noticed how unhappy Margaret was and he guessed the reasons why. He was heartbroken, but he had always taken whatever happened to him in life without fighting it, and so he sadly accepted that it had to be. Margaret did not mention that she intended to marry Ben, but Edwyn thought this could be likely. He could see that Ben held all the trump cards and could give Margaret what he could not – an affluent life, a beautiful home with staff to run it, plus a social life of leisure. Edwyn knew that Ben had sold his original Rolls Royce before the war and had bought a Daimler and now that the war was over he was about to buy a new Rolls. How could he compete with this? He could not, and Edwyn gave in with no more than a few protestations and moved out of their home. Although he would have loved to have kept in contact with Patricia, he knew she would be moving into a far superior life which he could not equal and so he did not ask for access to her.

At this point, Margaret said nothing to Patricia and she did not suspect anything.

The divorce was agreed and the decree nisi was granted in October 1947. When the decree absolute was issued a few weeks later, Margaret had to go to court in London. Patricia had a very sore throat that day and could not go to school but Margaret phoned her neighbour and asked if she would look after Patricia. She did not say she was going to London to finalise her divorce, but merely mentioned that she was meeting an old friend there. Patricia, wrapped in blankets to keep her warm, was taken to Margaret's neighbour. Margaret caught the train to London and then a taxi to Lincoln's Inn Fields, where the divorce case was being held. Happily, all the papers were in order, the court case lasted no more than ten minutes and Margaret came out of the building relieved that it was now over. Back home, she collected Patricia, who asked her what she had been doing. Margaret repeated her story that she had been meeting an old friend and Patricia seemed satisfied.

That evening Margaret put Patricia to bed as usual. It was two years since the war had ended, and Patricia was nine. She was just going to sleep when she heard the doorbell ring. This was unusual at night, and she heard her mother speaking quietly and then a man's low voice; so, determined to know who was there, she tiptoed down the stairs and sat three stairs up from the bottom of the staircase. The door of the lounge was open and she could see straight into the room to the fireplace on the far wall. Ben was standing on one side of the fireplace and her mother was standing on the other side. Patricia somehow sensed that something important was being said between them and she was dying to know what it was. All she could catch were some of the words that Ben was saying, something about '… and I will look after you and Patricia for the rest of my life…' She could not hear any more, and at that moment Margaret glanced up and saw her. She rushed out of the room, looking flushed, and hurried Patricia back to bed, telling her she must not come down again. Patricia determined to ask her mother in the morning what Uncle Ben had been saying.

At breakfast the next morning, she did not have to ask, as Margaret told her: 'We are going to marry Uncle Ben, and when we are married you must learn to call him Daddy.'

Strangely enough, this in no way astonished Patricia. She had lived with Ben for five years throughout the war and it was totally natural for her that he was always around; she had seen so little of her father during that time, and only lived with him for the two years since the war had ended.

The 'We' turned out to be a most significant word as, when speaking to Patricia, Margaret would refer to events either as 'Before we married Daddy, or 'After we married Daddy'.

'We' was also very much a clear indication that Ben had to take on not only a wife but also a daughter. In later years Patricia realised that her mother had married Ben on the condition that he paid for Patricia's clothes and private education, and many other things Margaret wanted her to have.

Over the next few weeks, Ben and Margaret looked for a suitable house in which they would all live. They settled on a huge Edwardian detached property in a quiet, unmade road between Bromley and Chislehurst. It was aptly named Greenacres, as the road leading up to it had fields on both sides. It had an in-and-out driveway and in the centre of the lawn in the front garden was a gigantic cream magnolia tree touched with pale pink. The house had two staircases; the main one had wide, shallow stairs and led up to the first-floor rooms – two large bedrooms, one on either side of the house, and three other rooms. One of these rooms was to be Patricia's bedroom and another her 'den', the third would be Ben's office. The second, narrower staircase was originally built for the servants, and led from the kitchen area onto the first floor, and then wound its way up again onto the second floor, where there were two more good-sized rooms.

The back garden was enormous and beautifully laid out. A lawn, large enough for a bowls pitch or tennis court, was to the far right with two greenhouses to the left. One of these was used for growing orchids and the other housed chrysanthemums and dahlias, all of which were brought into the house when they flowered, to provide cut flowers for the three ground-floor rooms. Margaret loved arranging these, as in India it was almost impossible for flowers to last very long in the heat. A vegetable patch was in front of the greenhouses and the front of the garden was paved in a semi-circular shape with lobelia and alyssum planted around it. In the centre of the paved area was an ornamental bird bath.

Very little time elapsed before Ben and Margaret were married, on 26 November, 1947; he was seventy-four and she was forty-seven. Ben had recently bought a new Rolls Royce, even more luxurious than the previous one that had met him on his return from Australia. The new Rolls took the three of them up to Westminster Chapel in London, where Margaret knew a minister who would marry divorced people, and Ben was in total agreement that the wedding would be held there. It was a quiet wedding with only Dr Crofton, now an elderly gentleman of Ben's age, and a friend of his as witnesses and, of course, Patricia. Afterwards Ben took everyone to the Trocadero restaurant in London's West End for roast beef with all the trimmings. He was in very good spirits and triumphant in finally having gained the lady he loved, the woman whom he had met nearly twenty years previously on the SS *Ragnera*. Surprisingly, Patricia took the wedding in her stride. She had hardly known her own father during the war years but had, of course, known Ben since she was a baby and he was also her godfather. The years of living with him in Leamington Spa during the war meant that Patricia was fully accustomed to him being around and it did not seem strange to her that her mother was now married to him.

For Margaret, the marriage to Ben led to an immediate change of circumstances from a very modest life, when she had had to think of every penny, to one of luxury and social standing; very few people were living like this in the late 1940s.

Chapter 16

Greenacres and Great St Joans

It was a relief to Ben that he could leave it to Margaret to engage the staff for the new house; he knew she had lived with servants in India and would cope well with this. Having seen how her mother managed the servants in Darjeeling, Margaret had little trouble in doing this, and she knew what work would be needed for the upkeep of the big house. A month after the wedding, Ben, Margaret and Patricia moved into their new home. Cook was to live in and would have one of the two top bedrooms. She was called Doris and would be responsible for providing all the main meals, plus elevenses and tea for any other staff on the premises at the time. This could amount to a full table in the maid's sitting room, what with the 'dailies', Frankson the chauffeur, Milner the gardener, Evelyn Jones, Ben's secretary, plus anyone else around at the time.

Doris was a lady in her forties; she had never married and was never likely to now that she was confined to a kitchen in a house in a slightly out-of-the-way road. She was a jolly, cheerful person who would have loved to have got married and had a husband and children but had resigned herself now to remaining a spinster. Her only social contacts were with the other staff and the delivery boys who came from the butcher, baker, grocer and greengrocer. Margaret would come into the kitchen once a day to let her know what food was needed for the day, and to compile the orders for the delivery men. Apart from two half days off, Wednesdays and Sundays, Doris did not leave the house. Where she went on her half-days off, no one knew but she had to walk half a mile to get to the nearest bus stop. Cook's domain was sizeable and consisted of the kitchen, a generous larder, the maid's sitting room with a huge central table, a pantry with almost floor-length cupboards to store the china, plus a hatch through which the food was passed into the dining room.

Frankson was on call all day, and when he was not needed he worked in the garden. If he was required in the evenings to take Ben and Margaret either to the Bromley theatre or to London for a show or a dinner-dance, he was always given the afternoon off. He also looked after Pong the cat, acquired from a family known to Patricia, as their daughter was in the same class as her at school. Pong had a twin sister called Ping, whom the family had kept, and the two girls loved to laugh and talk about Ping-Pong. Frankson adored Pong and the first thing he did when he arrived in the morning was to feed him – Pong was always waiting for him, knowing his food was coming. Sadly, Pong died rather suddenly in middle-age and Frankson was broken-hearted, saying: 'That cat loved me; he knew he could depend on me and I fed him and looked after him, he was almost mine. No other cat will replace him.'

And no other cat did, as the household did not get another one.

Milner, the gardener, was employed full-time since the front and back gardens had so many different areas to them that there was always something to be done. Even in the cold winters he would go out and loosen the icy soil on the beds and mend any fences or paving stones that needed to be repaired.

Evelyn Jones worked in Ben's office every weekday morning until lunchtime; she had a small car and so didn't have the long walk to and from the house to the bus. A lady in her fifties, she was very plain and dumpy, had never married and never would. She did not say much, and usually took her tea at elevenses in Ben's office, as he liked to continue with his work without a break.

Greenacres's entrance hall housed a comfortable large corner seat next to a telephone table and two Black Forest bear carvings, one of a single bear with his front paws outstretched, which had been made into a chair, and the other, a long seat with a standing bear at each end. These carvings were so detailed that they even showed the way the fur grew on the bears. An ornamental gong, also of a dark carved wood, stood next to the long seat. The hall led through to the main staircase on the right, and just past this a door opened into a corridor, which led down to a loggia, from where the whole garden could be seen. Off the hall there was a morning room where the daily papers were put, and before long a television was installed there. This hefty machine resembled an enormous chest – when the lid was lifted the picture was reflected into it from the bottom part of the chest.

The rest of the ground floor consisted of two sizeable rooms, one being the lounge and the other the dining room. Margaret loved the lounge; she spent most of her time in it and had chosen many of the furnishings. Every time she opened the lounge door her eyes took in the lovely room. The grand piano, with its casing in Japanese lacquer, lent a certain grandeur to the room, as did the other pieces of lacquered furniture, either Japanese or Chinese – altogether there were eighteen. Amongst these were a settee and two armchairs, a two-tier desk with a wine cabinet below, a tall curio cabinet with four shelves filled with mementoes that Ben had collected abroad, a revolving bookcase, a coal scuttle, a coffee table, a clock for the mantelpiece and even a fender. Margaret had chosen brocade curtains in black with a pink and green Chinese design woven into them, and pink and green brocade seats for the lacquered settees and armchairs. A heavy Chinese rug in similar colours lay over the parquet floor in front of the fireplace, and a smaller one lay towards the bay window, which overlooked the garden. The mantelpiece held some choice pieces of Ben's, such as marble and Chinese porcelain figurines. The whole effect was sumptuous and yet the room had a graceful and comfortable feel to it.

Equally large, the dining room housed a huge, oval, mahogany table and an enormous sideboard to match. On the sideboard was a collection of silver, ranging from a salver which held two teapots and all the necessary items for tea, plus two ornate candlesticks, wine coolers, sauceboats and other small silver items. As in the drawing room, the curtains were brocade and the floor was covered in a fitted carpet in a beige and bronze tone.

When Margaret had first seen the house after the furniture had been delivered, she was completely overawed by it. She had never been in a house like it. Of course, the one in Leamington Spa had also been spacious and well-furnished, but it was rented and so the furniture was not Ben's, his furniture having been in storage throughout the war. This house was the perfect setting for Ben's possessions, and Margaret, with her appreciation of beautiful things, enjoyed arranging them to their best advantage. When Ben's furniture for the drawing room was delivered she had asked him: 'Where would you like the sofa put, and the armchairs and the different pieces of Chinese lacquer and ornaments?'

And Ben, more than happy to let Margaret decide these things for him, told her: 'You put them where you think is best, darling, and do this for all the other rooms too. I know you have a natural talent for making a home comfortable and attractive.'

Margaret, delighted to be free to arrange the rooms as she liked, replied: 'I would love to do this, and I'll try to make the house so that you'll be happy in it, and that it will be enjoyable for all who come here.'

'Thank you, darling, it's wonderful to think that you'll make this house a real home for us and we'll be able to entertain people here.'

Having Margaret to see to all the household needs freed Ben from his bachelor existence and allowed him to take pleasure in his home without any worries. Coping with the domestic concerns of the house came quite naturally to Margaret, as she only needed to oversee the work rather than having to do it herself. In truth, she was now living in a similar way to her mother, the difference being that the house and garden were immeasurably larger and grander than the house in Darjeeling. Apart from the handful of neighbouring large houses, the road had only a few minor roads around it, and being an unmade road it was never noisy or congested with traffic.

Margaret was pleased to find that three of Ben's nieces lived together in a house not far away in Bromley. She had met them before and rather enjoyed seeing them, as they were all kindly, warm-hearted women.

Both Margaret and Patricia soon got used to living at Greenacres. Margaret made sure Patricia was never noisy, especially when Ben slept between lunch and afternoon tea. He was amazingly tolerant of a child in the house, and never interfered with disciplining her – he left that to Margaret. She investigated the local schools, found one she liked about four miles away and took Patricia to see it. They were both impressed by the pleasant, airy classrooms set in substantial grounds, where games such as hockey, netball and rounders were played. Patricia could not wait to start at the school. 'Mummy, I really want to come here, please let me, and I can't wait to learn how to play hockey.'

Margaret smiled ruefully; Patricia's interest in sports astonished her since, apart from table tennis, Margaret was not a great sports fan. She remembered how Edwyn loved sport, especially tennis – he had won the tennis singles cup at the Bombay gymkhana in 1927. Watching Patricia, she had seen how she could outrace all her friends when they had races on the lawn at Greenacres.

'She has got this from her father,' she thought, and said: 'Of course you can come here. I'm more than happy with the school, and I'm sure you will do well, as I want you to go onto public school when you are about twelve.'

'Oh Mummy, Mummy, I'm so pleased, I want you to be proud of me.'

'I'm already proud of you, darling, very proud,' and Margaret felt overcome, as her daughter was by far and away the central focus of her life. She never forgot how she had had to give away her first daughter, and Patricia was now everything to her.

Ben paid for Patricia's education, and for her school uniform and anything else Margaret felt she required. Frankson drove her to and from school every day in the Daimler, unless she was going to tea with one of her friends, and he often drove Margaret to meet Patricia after school. If the Daimler was being serviced or had a problem, then Frankson took the Rolls. When this happened Patricia would offer lifts to any of her friends who were going home from school by bus, and to them this was a great occasion, to be driven in a Rolls Royce. She made friends easily and Margaret, ever conscious that Patricia was an only child, encouraged her to invite her friends back to Greenacres. They loved coming there and many years later they would still recall their visits. When tea was served, they would usually sit quietly, a bit overawed with the huge rooms and Japanese lacquered furniture. Ben was always there for afternoon tea and the girls could see he was much older than their own fathers. They went home to tell their parents all about their visits, and the parents tended to think it was a bit of an odd set-up but the girls just accepted everything.

Very soon after Ben and Margaret were married, in 1948 he had his seventy-fifth birthday. He was still fit, well and active and everyone could see how contented he was with his new wife. All his friends and nieces who lived nearby wanted to make an occasion of it. The staff at Greenacres got very excited too as they guessed there would be big celebrations. Margaret instructed Doris to make a huge fruit cake and ice it, and then put a 75-watt lamp on the top. All four nieces came for the birthday tea, as well as a few of Ben's friends, and there was much laughter, chatter and merriment. Only one of his nieces had children – three boys, who were all grown up now, but all three managed to arrive for the birthday tea since they always loved coming to Greenacres and seeing Uncle Ben. He enjoyed seeing them too and hearing about what they were doing. The eldest was teaching in a boy's school, the second was a photographer and the youngest was a trainee in a solicitor's firm in London. After tea was finished, a glass of Champagne was had by everyone and old times were happily recalled. Ben was keen to also celebrate this special birthday with just Margaret and Patricia, so he took them to the Dorchester hotel for a special lunch and told them they could choose anything they liked on the menu. Margaret reminded him of when they had met on the SS *Ragnera* and the ship had stopped in Marseille. Ben had taken her to a French restaurant where she had eaten mussels for the first time, followed by waffles, strawberries and a *petit suisse* cheese. Since then Margaret had always been interested in anything to do with France and its culture and so she chose a chicken dish with a cream sauce containing asparagus, mushrooms and peas. After eating it, she said it was the best dish she had ever eaten. Ben had a steak and Patricia choose roast lamb, which was carved for her from a huge trolley and presented with all the trimmings.

Christmases were often spent at the Bournemouth Hydro, a hotel that Dr Crofton had bought as an investment some years previously. He and Joyce were always there for Christmas, and Ben, Margaret and Patricia would frequently join them. Even Ben looked forward to the trip, as there was such a lot going on – games and competitions were arranged in the evenings, and of course a fabulous Christmas lunch was served on Christmas Day. Dr Crofton and Joyce were both happy to join with Ben, Margaret and Patricia to go to the local Anglican service; it was a joyful time, it did not seem to matter whether the individual members of the congregation believed in God or not, everyone was happy on Christmas Day.

On Boxing Day the hotel always had a Fancy Dress competition and in 1950 Margaret and Joyce decided to dress Patricia up as a little Dutch girl. Joyce got very excited about it since, having never married and not having any children of her own, she took a special interest in Patricia. She took her role as godmother very seriously, not only sending presents to Patricia but, more importantly, caring for her soul and spirit. She was relatively rigid in her religious beliefs and not open to other faiths or paths of thinking. Nevertheless, she had a certain understanding manner when relating to children, which they liked, and they felt at home in her company. She had brought some broderie anglaise with her – an open-weave cotton material patterned with tiny, embroidered holes. She measured Patricia and made a long skirt for her, then they added one of Patricia's school blouses, Margaret tied a patterned scarf around Patricia's chest and over that she wore a waistcoat. Altogether she looked quite the part. When the judging took place, she won first prize and was so proud of herself – she even remembered to thank Margaret and Joyce.

Margaret had wanted Patricia to go to public school and asked Jane Cullington, now nearly eighty, where she would recommend. Margaret and Jane had maintained their friendship for over twenty-five years and Margaret considered Jane's advice the very best. She recommended Great St Joans, a school with lovely grounds near a small town in West Dorset, surrounded by pretty Dorset villages. Ben paid for this, and willingly too – at this time the fees were £99 a term, but they went up to £101 a term a year later, which caused an outcry from the parents. When Margaret visited the school, she was impressed by the way the girls behaved and the Christian faith promoted there. Since having baby Grace her Catholic faith had waned, but with the influence of her Brethren friends and the meetings she had attended at the local Anglican church, she wanted a school with a Christian foundation. Patricia was put down for the school and started there in January 1951 when she was twelve. Not having had brothers or sisters, living in a dormitory should have seemed odd to an only child, but she took to it with ease, the advantage being that she had companions now. After having had running water in the rooms at Greenacres, she found it a trifle strange to have to take a jug to the sluice room to collect the hot water for washing every morning since there were no baths. Patricia settled down there with no trouble and the routine of the school suited her, as she liked to know what was expected of her, and the times when things were meant to happen.

During her time at Great St Joans, Patricia excelled in maths and sport and was in the school teams for both lacrosse and tennis. During the school holidays Ben had bought her a Kum-Bak – a tennis training aid. It consisted of a ball attached to a racket with strong elastic, which could be hit over the net and was then returned. It was great fun and Patricia let all her friends have a go at this. When Latin was offered on the curriculum she begged Margaret to let her take it, but Margaret, knowing how she herself had suffered with her lack of domestic knowledge when she came over to England, said she must take Domestic Science. 'Darling, I don't want you to go through what I did, and nowadays you can't get staff easily, and people have to do their own work.'

'But, Mummy, I really love Latin; it is such a logical language and so easy to learn, and I don't like the idea of cooking and sewing.'

'I know,' said Margaret, 'but when you get married you will have to get down to practical things like these to run your home properly.'

'I don't think I will get married,' said Patricia.

'You will, darling, and I hope you will marry a good man who'll be relatively wealthy.'

'So do I.'

And so, Margaret insisted on Patricia taking Domestic Science, but when she sat her GCE 'O' Level examination for this, she was in disgrace, as she was the first person ever in the school to have failed the subject.

Exeats were permitted for only two weekends a term and pupils were not allowed to go home unless they lived nearby but could go out only for meals locally. The nearest good hotel was the Mill on the Stream, not too far from Charmouth. Ben and Margaret always stayed there when they came to see Patricia, so that they would be close to the school. Margaret longed to be with her daughter and each time she counted the days until the exeats were due. The Hare and Hounds had a large lounge with comfortable sofas, where Ben would have his afternoon siesta after their lunch. To Margaret's great delight, on their second visit there she discovered two table tennis tables on the second floor of the hotel. From then on, she and Patricia would have many games there. Margaret had previously taught Patricia how to play and she watched her daughter gradually improve; Margaret, of course, had never forgotten her former skill. By the time Patricia left Great St Joans they were equally good, and they would escape to the table tennis area every time Patricia had an exeat. Many battles were fought, to the amusement of onlookers, and the two of them had immense fun doing this.

The girls had to write to their parents every Sunday, and Patricia wrote home on Tuesdays as well. The school routine was hardly news, so she told her mother about the sports. Patricia had followed in her father's footsteps and she excelled at both lacrosse, tennis and gymnastics. Detailed reports of matches she had played and how she was the only one who had leapt over the buck and the horse were recounted in the letters. Although sport, apart from table tennis, held little interest for Margaret, she treasured these letters and years later she showed Patricia the huge bundle of them she had kept in a shoe box. 'These are all the letters you wrote to me from Great St Joans, darling. Have a look at some of them.'

Picking up a few, Patricia had glanced through them, and realising how repetitive they were, mostly describing lacrosse or tennis matches, she said: 'Mummy, have you really kept them all this time. I'm amazed, I can see now how uninteresting they must have been for you.'

'Maybe, but each letter you wrote kept me in touch with you. I know that most of the girls only wrote home on Sundays, but you wrote on Tuesdays too, I can't tell you how much that meant to me. Knowing that you would write another letter to me on Tuesdays was something I looked forward to.'

It was during Patricia's time at Great St Joans that George VI died unexpectedly. All the girls could talk about in the first half of 1953 was the forthcoming coronation of Elizabeth, his daughter, which was to take place on 2 June, fifteen months after the death of the King. The excitement mounted in the school and leave of absence was granted for four days. Patricia came home on the train to London and was met by Margaret in the Rolls. The coronation was without doubt the most notable event of the year, probably of the decade, and in the weeks leading up it, sales of television sets increased considerably. Many of Ben and Margaret's neighbours and friends had no televisions and so they invited about twenty of them to view this significant occasion. The staff at Greenacres were busy the week before bringing in chairs from all the other rooms in the house to the morning room where everyone would watch the service. Cook had worked hard to make a special cake – a fruit cake, the top decorated with glacé icing and the figure of the young Queen sitting on a throne; she had modelled this from sugar paste, using food colourings to tint the various parts, and the paste had hardened and kept its shape. Everyone had a slice and said how clever Cook had been and she revelled in their admiration. After viewing the coronation, Ben produced Champagne for his guests and with great enthusiasm they all toasted the new Queen.

Soon after her marriage to Ben, Margaret had joined the local Anglican church and she had persuaded him to go to the Sunday morning service with her. Attending church weekly may or may not have given Ben a belief in God, but he showed his generosity in other ways. He paid for the vicar and his wife to go on holiday every year, he took them to the Wimbledon tennis finals and invited them to his house to see the Oxford and Cambridge Boat Race on television.

Ben was a generous person; he had made a lot of money but his relatives, although far from being poor, were not wealthy. He would regularly invite his three nieces, who lived nearby, and their sister, who lived in Brighton, over for lunch. At Christmastime he told Margaret to buy them all good presents. For Margaret, her membership of the church was a vital part of her life. The congregation all knew Ben was wealthy, as the vicar had no compunction about letting them know about Ben's kindness towards him and his wife. Ben and Margaret were regarded as a somewhat unusual couple by the congregation, yet their genuineness was appreciated.

Patricia had started at boarding school, and this gave Margaret the freedom to meet Janice and Ingrid during the day. Janice was now living in Wimbledon and Ingrid was in Richmond. Janice had five children, four girls and a boy. Whenever John, her doctor husband, had to visit patients in their homes, she needed to stay in to take his phone calls and so Margaret would go over to Wimbledon to see her. Their house was a large building with John's surgery and waiting room on the ground floor. Margaret wondered how on earth Janice coped with cooking for five children, let alone cleaning this large house. Ingrid also had five children, surprisingly enough also four girls and a boy, the last two being twin girls. Ingrid could never get away; the washing, cooking, ironing and shopping had taken their toll on her and she had aged beyond her years. Yet she was still the same delightful lady Margaret had met before her marriage to Edwyn. When Ben and Margaret had gone on their honeymoon after their marriage, the Collins' had Patricia to stay for a week. Ingrid had trained her children to wipe their feet when they came into the house after playing outside but Patricia would go and play with them in the garden and never wipe her feet before going into the house. Poor Ingrid beseeched her to do this but it went in one ear and out of the other and by the end of the week Patricia was no better.

Surprisingly enough, it never once occurred to her that her childhood and upbringing were out of the ordinary. When she went to visit her friends' homes she merely accepted that this was the way their families lived. In fact, one of her friends, Gloria, lived in an apartment on the second floor. For Patricia, climbing two flights of stairs to get there was an adventure that knew no bounds. Gloria's parents were almost bohemian in their lives and allowed their two children to 'express' themselves, which meant noise and shouting abounded. Patricia joined in with delight, but when Margaret came to collect her and saw the commotion and the untidy room she was horrified and told Patricia she did not want her to go there again. Margaret's need to protect Patricia from temptation was almost heroic. Remorseful yet again about her own past failings, she was determined that her daughter should never be exposed to inducements that might lead her along an unsuitable pathway.

Chapter 17

Paris and Other Foreign Parts

When Patricia moved into the first year sixth class at Great St Joans, in autumn 1954, the question of GCE 'A' levels arose. Ben having been born in 1873 and Margaret having spent all her formative years in India, neither were keen for Patricia to continue her studies or to follow an academic life. Consequently, she was removed from the school in July 1955 and in September that year sent to a finishing school in Paris. This had not been chosen lightly, as one in Florence was also considered and the three of them had gone there to meet the Principal. If Florence was chosen, then Patricia would learn Italian. The imposing finishing school there had a certain grandeur and the Signora seemed a very affluent and cultured lady. Afternoon tea was served from an ornate trolley but with only cream, and not milk, for the tea. Patricia never drank tea and having to drink it loaded with cream quite put her off. Margaret too felt the atmosphere was far too stilted and severe.

They then went to Paris to meet the Principal of another finishing school. This time Madame was much more genial and outlined her plans for the girls in terms of showing them around the cultural sites of the city. She also employed a French tutor from the Sorbonne every morning to teach them French, and she seemed concerned to see her girls were happy. All three of them felt this was a much more relaxed place, and of course Margaret loved the idea that Patricia would be in France and have the opportunity to absorb French culture. Madame Verlet's school was chosen and Patricia left Great St Joans at the end of the first year sixth and spent six months in Paris, coming home only for the Christmas holidays.

Madame Verlet's home was in the 17th arrondissement, a stately building in a quiet but fashionable area. She took fourteen girls, all of whom were English apart from a Danish girl and an Arabic girl. Each room housed two girls, and Patricia shared with Anne, also an only child. It wasn't long before they became good friends and would go out together into the city.

Madame had explained how to travel on the métro or on the buses, and the girls soon understood this. She took good care to frequently remind the girls how to behave: *'Mes enfants, il vous devez toujours être poli,'*, meaning they must always be polite. Behaviour at meals was also watched, as Madame employed a butler, Lucien, to serve at table. Margaret was all for this, she considered good manners to be essential. For Patricia to be able to speak French and to soak up the finest French culture was just what Margaret wanted for her. She was delighted with Madame Verlet, as it seemed that Madame held the same values as herself.

The afternoons were spent either going to the principal museums and art galleries or they were free. If the girls wanted to go out in the evenings they needed permission from Madame and she needed to speak on the phone with the person they were going to see. Madame was a charming, well-dressed and intelligent lady 'of a certain age' who occasionally took the girls out in the evening to a play or the opera. No one ever knew her Christian name. Her only child, a daughter called Francoise, lived with her and was engaged to a Canadian, Pierre, whom Madame violently disapproved of.

Patricia would write home excitedly about her time in Paris. 'Madamoiselle Carlotti comes every morning for French tuition. She gives us a short dictation every day. I find it quite interesting to try and guess how the words are spelt, but most of the girls make no effort. Some of them have not even got O-level French, and when she asks them to spell a word they just shrug their shoulders. At least I do try.'

Another letter: 'Madame took us all to the Opera Garnier last night; it is a huge, impressive building and holds nearly 2,000 people. It was such a grand occasion, we all had to wear our very best dresses. The opera was *Manon*; it was sung in French and had five acts, and Madame told us she had chosen it as the shorter five acts made it easier for us to understand. I don't think any of us understood much of the French, but the whole thing was so impressive and you could sense the emotion of the singers. The costumes were richly embroidered and when the main singers were not singing the chorus sang in perfect unison.'

A later letter: 'Anne and I went to Montmartre today. We did not take the *petit train* but walked up the long steps, as Montmartre is on a hill. Once you get there you are in another world, a world of artists and interesting smaller houses, plus the Sacré-Coeur cathedral, an imposing white building known to be the highest point in Paris. From here you can look down and get an amazing view of the city. Artists were in the streets trying to sell their work or trying to persuade you to let them draw or paint your portrait. Such interesting people to talk to and such a happy atmosphere. Anne and I sat in a café for an hour and watched the life there, it is so different from the fashionable areas of Paris we usually spend our time in. I really want to go again but am not sure Anne is so keen.'

Margaret lived for Patricia's letters from Paris, they were a breath of fresh air to her. Once a term Ben and she would fly over to Paris for the weekend and take Patricia out. As the girls had been educated by Madame about high-quality French food, they were all keen on going to the top Paris restaurants. Madame recommended Antoine's, and Patricia begged to go there to eat snails. The snails arrived soused in garlic butter, which neither Ben, Margaret nor Patricia greatly took to, but the experience of dining at this superb restaurant was a well-remembered occasion. The restaurant survives today, still noted for its excellent food.

Ben never interfered with how Margaret brought Patricia up. He had lived in London for many years and knew all the best restaurants and hotels. After the war, he had invested in property and from time to time he needed to visit his rental properties there to ensure that they were kept in good order, so he would take Margaret and they would then go on to have lunch in London. They liked to go to Veeraswamys, a noted Indian restaurant overlooking Regent Street, where the very best authentic curries were served, or Simpsons in the Strand, which was known as a celebrated venue and a 'temple of food'. Simpsons was famous for always having a gigantic trolley of succulent roast beef, accompanied by crispy roast potatoes and several vegetables. In the school holidays Patricia had always been taken with them and she grew up thinking it was normal to go to the best hotels and restaurants. In fact, Ben had once said to her jokingly: 'I think you believe money grows on trees!'

He spoke true words – Patricia's upbringing did not fit her for the reality of life. Margaret had protected her from learning about so many of the practical tasks that adults need to know and become competent at: the ability to earn a living in order to cope financially and the domestic skills needed for running a home were unknown to her. Despite the years she had been married to Edwyn, Margaret had never learnt to cope with household chores – her abilities and talents lay in a different direction and she tended to avoid the tasks she found more demanding to get done. For Margaret, the absence of any guidance about practical matters started in her infancy and remained a problem for her all her life. Thus, she was totally unable to pass on any practical knowledge to Patricia, as Patricia had spent nearly all her childhood living in luxury, protected by Ben's wealth.

Margaret had never learned to drive – she had never needed to, as whenever she wanted to go out Frankson would drive her, to visit friends or go into Bromley to shop, and collect her. But when Patricia was seventeen, she had driving lessons and passed her test and Ben let her use the Daimler whenever she wanted. She was quite competent and would visit her friends or drive into Bromley to meet one of them at the Coffee Importers for coffee. The aroma emanating from the premises where the coffee beans were ground suffused the whole road, and the shop was a landmark in the town. Patricia would also take the Daimler frequently to the local tennis club. The one thing Edwyn had excelled at was tennis and, knowing this, Margaret made sure that Patricia had tennis coaching from an early age. It paid off, as she was entered for the junior Queens tournament in London, when she was fourteen; however, she was eliminated halfway through the tournament by a girl two years older than her. She loved club tennis, as it was fun and she could go to the club at any time and find someone to play a game with. She would talk to Margaret about it a lot, and this pleased Margaret and made her thankful she had given Patricia the chance to follow her father at the one thing he had been good at.

On one occasion, the Daimler came to grief. Patricia was driving it to the tennis club down their unmade road, which was full of potholes, when she tried to avoid a very big hole, but the car hit the pothole and veered into a lamp post, which caused the glass at the top of it to shatter and gas to come out. The Daimler was also badly dented and Patricia was terrified that it would not move, but she very gingerly put it into gear and to her great relief she was able to drive it home. Scared of telling Ben what had happened, she told Margaret, and Margaret took it upon herself to tell Ben.

'Well, I was thinking of getting another car anyway!' he said.

The relief felt by both Margaret and Patricia was immense, and the new car duly arrived – a dark green Lanchester.

Ben and Margaret not only went to good restaurants, they also went abroad. The first trip they did was to Switzerland. Taking Patricia with them, they took the train from London, which passed through France during the night and went through to Vallorbe, the frontier into Switzerland. Ben had his own cabin and Margaret and Patricia, then ten years old, shared a cabin, Patricia demanding the top bunk. When the train stopped at Vallorbe for customs regulations, everybody got out to stretch their legs and an amusing incident occurred. On the platform a lady was offering liqueur chocolates to those in her vicinity and, before Margaret could stop her, she had given one to Patricia. When the liqueur from the chocolate shell spurted into her mouth, Patricia did not know what to do – it was an unpleasantly strong taste for her, and Margaret was rather disapproving of the lady who had offered it. The train then continued to Lucerne on the western shore of Lake Lucerne and the wonderfully fresh air of the lakeside was invigorating to them all.

Following their trip to Switzerland and once Patricia was at Great St Joans, Ben and Margaret had enjoyed other holidays abroad. The south of France and Nice were favourites of Margaret's and they established a habit of going there every January to escape the British winter. This was a particular treat for Margaret, as she had never forgotten her brief time in France during her passage on the SS *Ragnera*, when Ben had taken her on a tour of Marseille, followed by a delicious French meal. She sent postcards to Patricia at school from Austria, Switzerland and Nice and the other girls would think how romantic it was for her parents to be travelling abroad.

On one of their holidays in Nice, they made friends with another couple, Frederik and Ursula Weber, both of a similar age to Margaret. Frederik had been a lawyer, and they lived in Vienna. For three years after this they both booked at the same hotel and at the same time. Ursula was rather delicate and frail and she rested each afternoon, as of course did Ben. Frederik and Margaret would go for walks together, and slowly their relationship developed and their times together became precious, although nothing explicit was ever exchanged between them. Towards the end of Ben's life, in 1960 they were not able to continue going to Nice, and after he died Margaret received a postcard from Frederik from Nice, saying how much he missed the times they had spent together. A week later she received a small packet enclosing a tiny ring set with an opal shaped into a heart. There was no name on the packet, but she knew it was from Frederik. Margaret showed the ring to Patricia only after she was widowed, and when Patricia enquired who had sent it to her she said: 'It was just a man I knew.' Margaret had never seen Frederik again.

Margaret had time to be involved with charitable works, and she agreed to sit on several committees. However, not being practical, she would discuss with Ben the good work these charities were doing for the poor and needy, and he advised her and would inevitably donate money. Knowing that they would receive some finance from her, just about every committee approached Margaret. She was genuinely keen to help people, and she knew just how to tackle Ben when she felt a cause was close to her heart.

Ben belonged to one of the oldest City Livery companies, the Worshipful Company of Gold and Silver Wyre Drawers. Incorporated in 1623, it was granted Livery status in 1780 and its activities were largely charitable, contributing to those who had fallen on hard times. Dinner dances were held regularly throughout the winter months and Ben and Margaret were regular participants – the occasions were ceremonial, with superb table settings and an excellent dinner, followed by dancing. Ben loved the old-fashioned waltz, and whenever it was played he would get up immediately and dance with Margaret. He was energetic and fit throughout his eighties. Many of the older men looked at the couple and envied him his lovely charming wife.

Chapter 18

Life with Ben

Living in such an enormous house with a number of regular staff, Ben and Margaret quickly became well known and were considered a trifle unusual. The difference in age was observed and Margaret was criticised for marrying 'a sugar daddy'. But once people had met Margaret and seen what a warm and outgoing person she was, they changed their minds. The difficulty for her was that all the other women living nearby had husbands who were nearer their age who went out to work daily. She had to think twice before inviting anyone round for tea, as Ben always got up from his siesta for that, and he was not too pleased to find a lady there he did not know and once Ben came down for tea Margaret felt obliged to be with him for the rest of the day. Mornings were different – Ben's coffee and that of his secretary, Evelyn Jones, were taken up to his office.

As the years went by and Ben became older, Margaret did come to feel rather isolated. Since the house was on a secluded, unmade road, there were very few neighbours, but in due course she came to know some of them.

On one side of Greenacres was a house nearly as large. Betty Thornton, a spinster, lived there; it had previously been her parents' home. She was somewhat eccentric and would wander over in the summer months when she saw Ben and Margaret playing bowls on the lawn. She never sensed when it was right to leave and would hang on until she knew it was supper time, and Margaret felt obliged to invite her to join them for the meal. Margaret then had to hurry into the kitchen to ask Cook to find something to make the meal more substantial. Ben loved playing bowls in the summer months – he always had a good sleep after lunch and once he awoke he would be ready for a game. The lawn was mown frequently so that it was always short enough for the bowls to run along smoothly.

After supper Ben liked a game of cribbage. It took a while for Margaret to learn this game, and she never enjoyed it, but when Patricia was home from Great St Joans she was happy to play. Ben would be in high spirits and would gladly play all evening.

In March 1956 Patricia came home from her six months in Paris and Margaret was determined that the next step would be for her to be presented to the Queen. At first Ben thought this was unnecessary; he had well-connected associates with daughters but they had never considered it important to do this. However, Margaret gently insisted and finally persuaded him. This also meant that Patricia would have a coming-out party at one of the best hotels. Ben relented, provided that Margaret made all the arrangements.

In the 1950s certain formalities were required before a girl could be presented to the Queen. First, the girl had to have as her sponsor someone who had already been presented, as they would then be in a position to make the introduction. Fortunately, Margaret knew an elderly couple only three doors away from Greenacres whose daughter was married to one of Scotland's leading barristers, and she had already been presented at Court. Margaret was introduced to the daughter, Mrs Childhurst, who agreed to be Patricia's sponsor. Great plans were made for the Presentation and keen attention paid to the stipulated conditions – a cocktail dress reaching to mid-calf in a not-too-thin material was considered appropriate. Margaret dragged Patricia round a number of stores before she was prepared to buy her a cocktail dress in deep blue satin. An essential thing to be learnt was the Vacani curtsy, which required the girls to enter the room sideways, do a deep curtsy, with head up and hands by their sides, to the Queen, do the same to Prince Philip and then exit sideways, never turning their back on the Queen.

The day before the presentation, Ben, Margaret, Patricia and Mrs Childhurst stayed the night at a hotel in Westminster. Margaret was in a ferment of excitement and Mrs Childhurst was also excited, as she had never presented anyone at Court before. The next day, only Patricia and

Mrs Childhurst were allowed into the room for the Presentation; Ben and Margaret waited outside in an ante-room. The Queen and Prince Philip sat on throne-like chairs under a canopy, and when Mrs Childhurst later related this to her, Margaret was reminded of the British rule in India. All went well and the Vacani curtsy duly executed. Next, they all enjoyed a delicious tea with chocolate cake and, after the anxiety of performing the curtsy, the girls chattered excitedly and ate much cake… All the fathers and mothers were there, the mothers dressed in their very best and wearing their furs and the fathers wearing top hats – Ben had had to hire his. There were hundreds of girls presented in 1956 but the Presentations were stopped two years later. Those who had been presented to the Queen were now called debutantes.

The next event was Queen Charlotte's birthday ball, always held in Grosvenor House. Patricia, as all the debutantes did, had to dress in white. At the ball, a huge white cake was wheeled in, in front of which the debutantes performed their Vacani curtsy again. This ball signalled the start of the 'season' – a round of cocktail parties, dinners and dances, at which young debs of marriageable age socialised widely until, hopefully, they met the man they would marry. Margaret saw to it that Patricia was invited to a number of cocktail parties and coming-out dinner dances – the girls she had been with in Paris, some of her school friends and others they knew all invited her. These required a wardrobe of cocktail and evening dresses, for which Ben paid without demur.

Margaret persuaded Ben that Patricia's coming-out dinner dance should be at the Park Lane hotel. Eighty young people were invited, seated at tables for eight, with the addition of a table for Ben and Margaret and some of their closest friends.

After all the excitement of the season, life settled down. The idea of Patricia working did not enter Ben or Margaret's mind, even though her school friends and her local friends were all doing something. Some were becoming doctors, accountants and lawyers; others were less ambitious and training as nurses or secretaries, but no one just stayed at home. Patricia begged to be able to do something and finally Margaret allowed her to do a secretarial course in the mornings – only the mornings. All the other girls on the course stayed all day and so each morning the tutor would give Patricia the previous afternoon's work so that she could catch up on the work she had missed. Luckily, the tutor fully understood her situation and was sympathetic to her and each day he corrected the work she had done at home the previous afternoon.

When Patricia finished the course, she had precious little to do at home other than going up to London to meet friends. It was the time of the burgeoning of coffee houses, and the girls loved meeting there. One day she went up to meet an old school friend for lunch. Sue was working as a secretary and they met in her lunch hour. Sue prattled away about her job and Patricia came away feeling that her friend was at least doing something that was earning her money. Walking back down Regent Street to Charing Cross station for her train home, she passed the Swan and Edgar department store at Piccadilly Circus. Not being in a hurry, she went in and, on a whim, thought she would enquire about jobs there. She was directed to the personnel office and the lady in charge told her there was a job available in women's lingerie. Patricia found the department but was a bit nonplussed by the type of lingerie stocked there. However, she spoke to the lady in charge, who, after a brief interview, said she could start working part-time the following week. On her return home Patricia guessed her mother would not be pleased, but she knew she had to tell her.

'I was in Swan and Edgars today and I applied for a job there.'

'What on earth did you do that for? What is the job?' asked Margaret.

'It's in the lingerie department,' replied Patricia.

'The lingerie department of Swan and Edgars!'

'Yes.'

'Darling, what on earth got into you?' said Margaret. 'There is no way you can go and work there. I will phone them tomorrow and explain that it was a mistake.'

Patricia was dismayed. 'Mummy, I want to do something, not just stay at home all the time.'

'I know darling, but I am hoping that with all these parties you go to you will meet someone suitable to marry.'

What Margaret did not know was that Patricia at this time was not at all enthusiastic about the socialising and it was not unusual for her to stand on the edge of a room at cocktail parties and hardly exchange a word with anyone. Tongue-tied and uneasy at these events, she was only comfortable with her girlfriends.

Swan and Edgar were phoned in the morning by Margaret, and the lady she spoke to said they quite understood, as they had thought Patricia was not the usual type of girl to apply for a sales position in the lingerie department. Ben had smiled ruefully when told the story, but had secretly thought Patricia had at least some initiative, although he did not mention this to Margaret.

And so, life continued until a contemporary friend of Margaret's asked if she could take Patricia for a week to a Christian conference centre. Margaret's faith, which had renewed at the time when she was in touch with Dr Crofton again and his daughter Joyce, along with a number of other Christian people they had introduced her to, had somewhat waned since her marriage to Ben, although she still attended church. Hearing of this conference centre in Kent she was not against Patricia going, and gave her consent.

On arriving at the conference centre with Margaret's friend, Patricia was surprised to find that most of the people there were young. Some of them had been before and at supper there was a lot of laughing and easy camaraderie and she felt at ease in the atmosphere. After supper the owner of the centre spoke briefly about what would happen during the week. It would be both fun and serious. There would be games of all sorts, quizzes and merriment but there would also be some thought-provoking, serious and significant talks. The whole atmosphere was one of happiness, sustained by a belief in God which gave a meaning to life. This caught Patricia at a time when, not having a training or job to go to, she found little purpose in her life, and she very quickly felt comfortable with the beliefs held there. As the week progressed, she made friendships with girls that were to last for many years and without doubt it was a time of change for her – she had found a direction and a base for her future life.

She returned home with a firm faith. Brimming with a new confidence and what she felt to be an enduring commitment to God, she told Margaret, who admitted that although she went to church every Sunday it had become rather mechanical but now that Patricia was so keen, she herself wanted to become a more ardent Christian.

They joined the local evangelical church and found it a welcoming place. Margaret became a regular committed member of the women's group in the church and it was a support to her as Ben got older and she had less freedom.

Patricia joined the Young Peoples' Fellowship, where she also found friends and became a keen and eager member of the group. Having done the secretarial course, she took on the job of secretary for the group and would write up the times of meetings and any other activities arranged by them. It was at this time that she met a young, well-to-do, Jewish man at one of the London parties. He took her out several times and she felt that here was someone she could get on well with – he was keen on her and took her to meet his parents. Patricia explained to him that she was a Christian and what it meant to her, but he found it hard to understand her commitment, so she persuaded him to go with her to a film about Billy Graham, the evangelist. He watched the film carefully but was still unconvinced, so with a certain reluctance she told him she could not see him again – the relationship could not progress if they didn't share the same faith. On returning home she told Margaret what had happened, and Margaret was caught between empathising with her daughter but at the same time feeling Patricia had turned down the possibility of a wealthy marriage.

Chapter 19

Renewed Faith, and Patricia's Wedding

In 1958 when Patricia was twenty, a young man joined the Young Peoples' Fellowship group. At that time nearly all the members were in their late teens or early twenties – Malcolm was nearly thirty.

He had been brought up to attend and be part of the local Plymouth Brethren meeting, which his father, Geoffrey Harding, had led for many years. His mother was the daughter of an Anglican vicar and was not always comfortable with the Brethren way of doing things but felt she must support her husband. Malcolm was one of four children, all of whom eventually became Anglicans. Being slightly older than most of the group, he was rapidly appointed the leader. Very soon after this he wrote Patricia a note saying he needed to look for a location where the group could have a walk and a day out together in the Kent countryside, and would she please help him with this. She agreed to do so and, a few days later, he picked her up in his TR2 racing green sports car. As they drove into Kent, he suggested that once they'd found a good location for the day out, they have lunch somewhere. She had not expected this, but happily agreed and as they drove they talked a lot about the group and about their faith.

'Sunday is a special day for me,' he confided.

'Oh, it is for me too,' responded Patricia, pleased to find a kindred spirit.

'I like to go to church twice, morning and evening.'

'I do too,' said Patricia, 'and my mother would like to come in the evenings, but she feels she cannot leave my stepfather – he is in his eighties now.'

During lunch, they talked about their families and then, when he dropped her off at her house, Malcolm asked to see her again. He took her out to dinner twice and they found they got on both spiritually and as individuals. Patricia then invited him over to dinner to meet Ben and Margaret, who were both most impressed with him, since he came from a wealthy background and had a job with good prospects. The second time he came to dinner, he and Patricia went up to her 'den' afterwards and carried on talking. Then, before he left, he proposed and Patricia accepted him willingly; they both felt it was right in the eyes of God. Ben and Margaret had gone to bed by this time, but Patricia wanted to tell Margaret her good news and crept into their bedroom, where she found Margaret still awake. So as not to wake Ben, she kept her voice low. Margaret was rather surprised at the news, as they had not known each other for long, but she was more than satisfied that Malcolm was not only a Christian but that he also came from a well-to-do family who lived in a house commensurate with Greenacres. He had mentioned his father's role in the Plymouth Brethren and, of course, Margaret had previously had many links with them through Dr Crofton, Joyce, Janice and Ingrid, all of whom she kept in touch with.

Without delay, Margaret invited Malcolm and his parents over for lunch so that the two families could meet. Ben, Margaret and Patricia were of course invited back, and it seemed that both families were equally thrilled about the engagement. Ben was extremely pleased to see that Margaret was happy about the marriage, and realised it was going to be an expensive time for him…

Malcolm's mother expressed enthusiasm to Margaret: 'We are both so pleased that Malcolm has found such a delightful young lady like your Patricia. We had been wondering if he would ever find a suitable wife, and she seems just right for him.'

And Margaret, equally gratified, did not hide her pleasure. 'Ben and I are delighted too. Malcolm has been over to our place several times and now that we have got to know him, we like him very much.'

Malcolm's father told Margaret that Malcolm's job had excellent prospects – he was the personnel director of a well-known metal company – and Ben was relieved that Patricia would be marrying into a wealthy family, and that Malcolm would have enough from his salary to pay for all the household expenses.

Malcolm took Patricia to a Bond Street jeweller to choose the engagement ring, and they decided on a three-stone diamond. Admittedly, Patricia felt she had been somewhat rushed into the engagement and arrangements towards the marriage were moving very fast, but her upbringing had persuaded her that this is what you did – you found a good man and married him.

The forthcoming marriage sent Margaret full tilt into the wedding preparations. Where should they shop for the dress? At which church should it be? Which guests should be invited and at which hotel should the reception be held? Poor Ben was kept abreast of every single minute detail and Greenacres was a frenzy of preparations. Margaret favoured St Margaret's, Westminster for the service. Known as 'the church on Parliament Square', it is sited next door to Westminster Abbey and was a favoured venue for society weddings. Planning the service with the Rector took some time to get it just as she wanted. Patricia was happy to leave everything to her; she just felt that Margaret knew best – she would fit in with whatever was arranged. Once this was decided, the choice of bridesmaids loomed.

'I must have Rosemary,' said Patricia. 'We are best friends and have known each other since we were eight, and we know the family. And I would like to have Anne, my friend from Paris.'

Margaret agreed – Rosemary was Janice's eldest daughter, nine months younger than Patricia. 'However,' she said, 'Diana, Ruth and Jean are your closest friends here and so you should have them, but the bridesmaids must go up the aisle in two's, so have only Diana and Ruth.'

Patricia wanted Jean too but saw the logic in her mother's argument and gave way.

'Good,' said Margaret, 'and what about small bridesmaids?' The Collins twins are nearly nine now and they would be perfect. They are old enough to behave and not cause a commotion.'

The Collins twins were the daughters of Margaret's long-standing friend Ingrid Collins. Patricia happily agreed and phoned her four friends, who were all honoured to be asked. Margaret phoned Ingrid Collins, who was immensely flattered that her children had been chosen to be bridesmaids at such a notable church as St Margaret's, Westminster. Then she phoned Janice, who had heard the news from Rosemary and was also thrilled.

Jane Cullington had kept up with Margaret all this time and they had known each other for over thirty years. Now in her early eighties, she was a tower of strength to Margaret and advised her about everything. She had supported Margaret during her divorce from Edwyn, encouraged her to marry Ben and to aim for the best life for her and Patricia. She knew all the very best places in London to hold weddings and celebrations – she had suggested the Park Lane hotel for Patricia's coming-out party and now she advised that the Dorchester hotel would be perfect for her wedding reception. Margaret agreed; she had thought of the Dorchester herself. Ben, of course, was consulted about everything – as he was paying for it all – but Margaret was so keen on getting precise details right that he left it all to her, merely asking for the cost of everything and meekly agreeing. The room at the Dorchester was chosen, the number of guests planned and the size of the tables they would sit at agreed upon. Long conversations were held at Greenacres as to who should be invited – Margaret was anxious not to hurt anyone's feelings. Margaret tried to include Ben in all the minutiae, as she wanted him to feel part of everything. However, he was now eighty-six and feeling his age and, in fact, was longing for a quiet life and looking forward to when all the fuss of the wedding would be over.

The next undertaking was to find the wedding dress and Margaret and Patricia duly visited all the big London stores – and got remarkably tired. Eventually, a saleslady in Dickins and Jones pointed out that Patricia looked better in cream than white, and she produced a cream brocade dress with a gold thread running through it. Margaret saw at once how well it suited her daughter. After three fittings, necessitating a trip to London each time, the dress fitted perfectly.

Malcolm and Patricia were now looking for a house in the area, and eventually the perfect house was found, convenient for Malcolm's work and close to both sets of parents. Malcolm and Patricia discussed the honeymoon and decided on a small, unspoilt fishing village in the south of Spain. Flights were booked from Heathrow, and finally all was in order for the wedding. Margaret was in both a state of excitement and of nerves. Seeing Patricia married at St Margaret's, Westminster, followed by a reception at the Dorchester hotel was the pinnacle of her dreams. She thought back to her childhood in Darjeeling and how happy this had been, but as always the relationship with Gordon clouded her thoughts as she recalled the utter misery of having to give up baby Grace.

'I have never forgotten that little face,' she thought. 'She would be over thirty now. I can't stop wondering what has happened to her and what her life is like now. In fact, I could possibly have grandchildren, as she is ten years older than Patricia, but I will never know.'

With an immense effort, Margaret deliberately turned her mind back to the wedding plans.

It was September, 1959, and the day of the wedding arrived. Frankson drove Ben and Patricia in the Rolls Royce to St Margaret's, Westminster. He had spent days making sure the inside was spotlessly clean and the outside shining and for weeks afterwards he related the events of the day to the staff at Greenacres. Everything went remarkably smoothly – Patricia looked lovely in her dress as Ben walked her up the aisle, and Margaret revelled in it all. After the sumptuous reception, they all gathered outside the Dorchester to wish Malcolm and Patricia well as they set off on their honeymoon.

Margaret, determined to get on with Malcolm's family, especially his mother, insisted on letting her meet them at the airport when they returned from honeymoon but was keen to know all about Calella de Palafrugell, the fishing village in southern Spain they had been to.

After the build-up to the wedding, Ben was feeling his age and wanted nothing but a return to normality and a more calm and peaceful life. But now that Patricia was married, Margaret saw less of her and started to feel somewhat alone in the big house. Malcolm and Patricia spent alternate Sundays with them and she lived for this.

Ben had never been a particularly talkative man, and now he retreated into himself even more. He simply wanted to quietly enjoy the home and garden he had worked so hard for and his life with Margaret. However, Margaret, being so much younger, still needed some outside interests and although she saw Patricia regularly, as she lived nearby, Patricia was wrapped up in her new home and making friends with other young marrieds in the area.

Margaret depended a lot on her church meetings. Ben did not drive now but Frankson was still employed, so Margaret could go into Bromley to shop whenever she liked and go to her church meetings. Her faith in God was strengthened yet now something else started to worry her. Even though she could accept in theory that God forgave all sins, her thoughts were haunted by the feeling that He could not possibly forgive her personal sins, as they were so great. Having to spend more time at home now with Ben, she had not enough to do to banish these unhappy feelings, and every day they weighed her down. She could not talk to Ben about this, as she had never told him about the affair.

Evenings passed either in playing cribbage or with Ben dozing in his armchair and Margaret going over and over in her mind the regrettable time with Gordon. She wondered if he had ever thought of his baby, and that he might even have grandchildren now. At times she thought about getting in contact with him, but she had no idea how to do this, and very likely he might not still be in Darjeeling, in which case there was no hope of accomplishing this.

The months went by very slowly for Margaret and she hoped that Patricia would have a baby. Ben had never had a son and he had no grandchildren that he knew of, since nothing had been heard of from Dorothy since she'd gone to the States. From time to time he would say to Patricia: 'When's the little boy coming along?' Sadly, he would never see Patricia's son.

Chapter 20

Ben Dies, and a New Beginning

It was almost inevitable that Ben would die before Margaret, as there was nearly thirty years between them. In fact, he sailed through his eighties, travelling abroad, going to City Livery dinner-dances and generally living a fit and normal life. His ninetieth birthday celebrations came and went and Margaret made sure he had a magnificent cake, but when she next saw Patricia she confided that Ben was getting very slow and finding life a bit wearisome. A year later, in 1963, he went out to post a business letter and, just as he was putting the letter into the box, he collapsed. Fortunately, Margaret was with him, as she never let him go out alone now. Ben could not get up and could barely speak, but Margaret had to leave him on the pavement while she went into the nearest house to phone for an ambulance. It was not long in coming and Ben was gently lifted into the vehicle and taken to hospital, accompanied by Margaret, both in a state of shock. He said he was in pain in his left leg and was then admitted to the geriatric ward. An x-ray was taken but it was the next day before the results were known – Ben had broken his left femur. This sudden turn of events left Margaret alarmed, as she was so used to relying practically on Ben and to him being in good health; his accident left her feeling anxious as to how she would cope when he came home.

Four days later an ambulance brought Ben home; he was barely able to walk even though he had been given two sticks to support himself. The ambulance men carried him up the stairs on a hospital chair and into the bedroom. He was obvious very frail and did not say much. Margaret had told his three nieces who lived nearby about the fall, and the eldest, Eileen, who had been a midwife, was totally knowledgeable about what was needed and said she would come in every day to help Margaret. Margaret assured her that Frankson would collect her and take her home, as Greenacres was not the easiest place to get to without a car. Eileen kept her word and came in every day, staying from mid-morning until late afternoon. Several days went by and Ben made little progress; it seemed that rather than getting stronger he was declining, and by the sixth day he was in bed the whole time and saying very little.

Margaret asked Eileen: 'How is he today? He does not seem too good. Do you think he is going to get well again?'

Eileen, knowing Margaret's total lack of nursing skills, and not wishing to alarm her replied: 'It is difficult to say; we should know in a couple of days. But I will continue coming, as I know you need me.'

'I certainly do,' said Margaret.

Indeed, she did. It was not just the nursing that troubled her – she dreaded that Ben might become a vegetable and unable to communicate with her, although he was barely speaking now. However, he did not seem in pain and he did not complain.

Margaret had to be content with this explanation and she hovered between wanting Ben to get well and fit again and feeling certain she would be unable to cope if he became a complete invalid.

Cook always brought the morning coffee up to the bedroom for Margaret and Eileen and saw perfectly well how ill Ben was, and she regaled the staff with this news during elevenses in the Maids' Sitting Room where they gathered. There was a state of uncertainty in the house since, knowing that Ben had passed his ninetieth birthday the previous year, they all wondered what would happen if he had to go into a nursing home or died. It was evident that Margaret would not stay on in this huge house and garden on her own. Cook said: 'I'll be the first to go. Madam won't need me if she's on her own. At my age I don't know if I'll find another job. I've been here now for fifteen years. I just hope he recovers.'

Frankson responded: 'Madam does not drive, but I'm sure she will not keep me on if he dies. Like you, I've been here for fifteen years.'

Milner, the gardener, also voiced his anxiety: 'I doubt if she will stay on here if he dies, I work full-time here and there are not many families now who have the money to employ a gardener full-time. I guess it would be the end for me.'

Evelyn Jones, Ben's secretary, had not been coming since the accident, but she did come in four days after his return to see what was happening, and Margaret spoke with her: 'I have to tell you it is unlikely that Mr Charlton will be employing you again, but there is nothing definite at the moment, and if he has to let you go I will give you a good reference.'

Evelyn repeated this to the staff in the Maids' Sitting Room and they all felt things did not look good for them.

Eileen had never married and had worked full-time as a midwife at Bromley hospital for over forty years, and there was little she did not know from the experience she had gained. Seven days after Ben had come home, she recognised the signs that he was failing – he was not eating and was asleep much of the time. She did not want to blatantly tell Margaret this, but at the same time she did not want to hide it from her, so she simply said nothing and carried on coming in every day to give Margaret some respite from looking after Ben.

Patricia had, of course, been told what had happened, and she visited on most days. Margaret found her presence supportive, as she could offload her anxious feelings onto her. Being so used to seeing Ben up and about and active all the years she had known him, Patricia found it discouraging to see him as he was – hardly awake and not able to eat. Having known him practically since her birth, her mind was not capable of imagining anything happening to him – he was someone who had always been there and very much part of her life and she was quite unable to visualise her life without him.

On the ninth day of Ben's return from hospital, Eileen saw the end coming, and she forewarned Margaret. Margaret came and sat by Ben's bedside and held his hand, he was unconscious, and his breathing was shallow. An hour later he slipped away very peacefully. Eileen knew exactly when and told Margaret. Her emotions were up and down – a minute before he had been alive and now, abruptly, it seemed he had gone, never to be recalled: this is the way death is, sudden and unchangeable, and when it happens we are always stunned.

For Margaret this was a massive shock, even though she had seen Ben weakening day after day since his collapse by the post box. Somehow she had felt he would return to the health he had always had. And now he was gone. Eileen phoned Patricia to say: 'Margaret needs you,' and she came over at once.

Equally saddened by his death, neither Margaret nor Patricia could take it in. Even after Margaret had arranged Ben's funeral, she still could not believe he had gone, but it became reality very quickly when she had to make decisions about what to do with the house, how to cope with bills coming in and what she should do with the rest of her life. Ben had seen to everything like this for the sixteen years they had been married. He seldom talked about money matters to her, judging it best 'not to bother her pretty little head', and as she had never understood these in any way she had been thankful she did not have to be involved with them. Knowing that he would almost certainly die before her, Ben had left all his money to her, appreciating that in turn she would leave it to Patricia.

'I cannot go on living in this huge house,' she thought. 'I must sell it and move to a smaller place and I will not need to keep the staff.'

Yet she panicked at these thoughts, as she knew the staff were her support system and the idea of running a home without them seemed like a nightmare. However, it had to be done, and the staff would have to go. Doris the cook, Frankson the chauffeur and Milner the gardener were all given notice. So was Evelyn Jones. Margaret had to explain to each one of them that she would be moving and not in need of their services, and as she did this she was overcome with a real feeling of compassion for them: none of them were young now and getting new employment would be hard. As well as this, all of them had served Ben and herself for years. She decided to give each of them a month's wages, which they appreciated, and all were provided with excellent references. After doing this, she felt worn out and alone; it was with the help of these people that she had been able to have the life she had had.

The Rolls and the Lanchester had to be sold – there was no way that Margaret could justify keeping them; there would not be enough work to employ a full-time chauffeur nor would she have been able to drive either of them, even if she could. She had got so used to being driven about in both cars for so many years that it was with genuine sadness that she parted with them. The large house had to be sold, but at least the couple who bought it were people she had previously known. Then there was the purchase of a new home. Margaret had no inkling of what type of property she should buy but eventually settled on a pleasant, four-bedroomed house in a quiet cul-de-sac of just twelve houses in Chislehurst. As she looked at Ben's possessions in the well-proportioned rooms at Greenacres, she sighed, knowing she would have to say goodbye to most of the furniture and Ben's collection of artefacts – in fact, all the familiar things she had got used to. She wandered from room to room planning what she would take to her new home and what she would send to auction.

'I don't know how I will cope in my new place,' she told Patricia. 'I feel very wobbly about the move. Ben saw to everything; I did not have to make any practical decisions and now I have to make them all on my own.'

Patricia looked at her mother and could see that she was flustered with so many things to think of before the move.

'Mum, I will help you over the move, and get you settled in. Once you are in your new home you'll feel a lot better. Make sure you take the things that you love so that you'll still have them with you.'

'I'm going to take driving lessons,' said Margaret. 'I'll have to, or I'll be stuck at home.'

'That's a good idea; you're only in your early sixties, it's not too late to learn and you need not drive far, just locally to get to your church meetings and your friends.'

Margaret felt that no one understood what a big change the move was for her. She thought of how much she had depended on Ben – not only during the years of their marriage, but also ever since she had met him on the SS *Ragnera* he had been there to guide her, and she had always had the feeling she could turn to him for help of any kind. Even when he was slower and declining in his late eighties, he still retained his sharp financial brain, and Margaret was able to talk through anything that bothered her. Now he was gone and as she reflected on her present life it seemed that the one person in the world on whom she had been able to depend had left her.

Margaret felt strongly about having given notice to Frankson. She did not drive and now that she had moved she had to take taxis every time she went out – shopping, visiting friends, getting to and from the Bible Study group were getting expensive. She decided to buy a small car and take her driving lessons in this rather than learn in the instructor's car. Margaret did not enjoy the lessons but persevered, as she knew what a bonus it would be once she passed the test. But driving did not come naturally to her, and the traffic around her bothered her. She sat the test and did not pass. After a few more lessons she sat the test once more and yet again she did not pass. Nearly in tears, she phoned Patricia who suggested she continue with her lessons and then have another try. And this time she passed! The first time she went out on her own after passing the test she felt very shaky and did not drive at more than twenty miles an hour. It was a while before she felt able to drive confidently, but she did have a new sense of freedom.

Chapter 21

A Grandchild, and Losing Money

Although she could now drive, Margaret was experiencing a lonely and disheartening time. Patricia was busy with her own home, and with entertaining Malcolm's colleagues, both in London and abroad. They were also very involved with the local Anglican church and Malcolm was training to be a lay preacher. However, they would often invite Margaret and Malcolm's parents to lunch on a Sunday, and Margaret looked forward to these occasions. Whenever Patricia phoned Margaret or called round, she could tell that her mother was struggling. Margaret's lifeline was her church and the women's meeting and she had also found another woman's group, which had been started by two dynamic ladies from the local Plymouth Brethren assembly. The group met weekly to study the Bible and to be a support to each other, especially to those who were going through a difficult time. Margaret was welcomed, and from the first meeting she knew she had come across a group of sincere and approachable women.

'We're so pleased to have you with us,' said Jennifer, one of the leaders.

'I do hope you will come again,' said Fiona, the other leader.

And Margaret, who was thinking they would not want her to join the group if they knew of her history, responded: 'I am very glad to be here today, Jennifer; I'm sure I'll come again.'

From that first meeting Margaret became a fervent member of the group – there was something that drew her in. She had a feeling they would accept whatever they were told and would never criticise or condemn.

Tempted to share her past with them, she still hung back and did not. The women liked her, she made an effort to please them and when there was a need for cakes or coffee she would always contribute something. Most of the women there had known of her before she joined the group, as Greenacres and the way it was run was familiar to most local people. Those who had not met Margaret before were surprised to find she was not snobbish but showed a genuine interest in their lives, even though these were less grand than hers. If neither of the leaders were able to have the meeting in their own homes, Margaret would invite the group to her house.

She was on good terms with Malcolm's mother, who had been able to recommend a lady who would come in to cook for her. Mrs Glazebrook was happy to serve the coffee to the group, and if some of them wondered why Margaret needed someone to simply make coffee and hand round the biscuits they did not say so. After all, Margaret was almost a legend locally. She also now had a cleaner, Mrs Pierre, who came twice a week.

Eventually, Patricia came round to tell Margaret she was pregnant. Margaret was ecstatic – at last, something to live for and take her attention away from brooding about the past. Here was something that would give her a real interest, she would be a grandmother.

She ordered an expensive pram for the baby and bought a mass of baby clothes but did this without consulting Patricia. Patricia then told her that Malcolm's mother would like to buy some of these things, and Margaret said: 'Maybe, but it is my daughter who is having the baby and naturally I want to buy baby clothes for her.'

'I know Mum, but it is Malcolm's baby too, so his family want to be involved, especially his mother.'

'But she has other grandchildren already,' countered Margaret.

'I know she has, but that doesn't mean that she feels this one is not important. I know it means a lot to her, as this will be the child of her eldest son.'

Margaret acquiesced, she had to, and she held back on buying any more baby clothes. But in her heart Patricia's baby was her own special grandchild and no one else's.

Malcolm booked Patricia into an exclusive nursing home in Welbeck Street in London and on 28 March, 1964 Patricia went into labour.

Malcolm phoned Margaret to let her know that labour had started. She was on her own at home and thoughts of something going wrong plagued her. Yet all went well and several hours later he phoned to let her know that a perfect baby boy had been born. Margaret was ecstatic, at last her own grandchild. The next day she took the train up to London to see Patricia and her new grandson. Thrilled at the sight of him she absorbed the privileged atmosphere of the nursing home and took it to be a good omen for his future.

'Isn't he tiny?' said Patricia. 'He is so small, I have to be very careful with him when I hold him.'

'Yes, he does seem small, yet he weighed nearly eight pounds, didn't he?'

'Yes, he did, seven pounds, nine ounces, a perfect size. He is crying quite a lot but apart from this he's fine.'

'Could I hold him, please?' asked Margaret.

'Of course you can, here he is.'

And Margaret held the little boy, who gazed up at her and won her heart for ever. They decided to name him after an Irish saint – Kevin.

Margaret prided herself on being a Granny, and when people told her how young she looked she blossomed. She felt her life was now worth living and her thoughts dwelt less on God not being able to forgive her.

Once Malcolm and Patricia were home with their son they engaged a live-in au pair, to help in the house and with babysitting. Patricia recovered well from the birth and was soon up and about but was pleased to have the help of another pair of hands. Malcolm had not been brought up to be involved with domestic tasks and he would leave them all to Patricia, who was not a lot better. Margaret, having grown up in India had never learnt to be practical, and had never taught the basic practical tasks to Patricia – once Margaret had married Ben neither she nor Patricia needed to be troubled with anything of that nature.

Both Margaret and Malcolm's mother called in from time to time to see their new grandson, and slowly a routine was established. Margaret's friends, especially those from the Bible Study group, were regaled interminably about Kevin's progress. Margaret had, however, fixed ideas on how he should be brought up – how his hair should be cut, what trousers he should wear and what he should or should not be playing with. Malcolm and Patricia listened calmly and then went their own ways…

Having an au pair allowed Patricia and Malcolm to go out in the evening and at weekends. They were both staunch members of the local evangelical church, the same church to which Margaret belonged, and they were able to get involved with many of the local church activities Malcolm's father was still the leader of the Plymouth Brethren meeting nearby and his mother continued to belong to the meeting there. Patricia could also be available, as Malcolm's wife, whenever needed to go to business dinners or entertain the company's foreign guests or colleagues from the States. The company chauffeur was always on hand to drive her and the guests whenever needed.

Distracted by the focus on her grandson, Margaret now found herself responsible for managing Ben's money. When probate had been granted, Ben's executor, his solicitor, had passed all the money over to Margaret. It was not just in a lump sum but also comprised investments in a number of companies, some of which paid dividends, and she found she had enough money coming in for all she needed. As time went by, however, she noticed that the dividends were becoming noticeably smaller, with the result that she had less money. Having no idea whatsoever how to restructure her investments, she became flustered, thinking her money was dwindling. Not wishing to divulge her problems to other people, she did nothing for a few months. Finally, in desperation she confided in a very close old friend who was married to a retired accountant. Frances assured Margaret that her husband would sort everything out for her: 'Don't worry, Margaret. Harold knows all about investments; he will look through everything and put it all in order so that it is simple for you to cope with.'

Margaret felt that a huge burden had rolled off her shoulders. 'Thank you so, so much; what a relief to find Harold will resolve any concerns and put things in order for me,' she said.

'He will be happy to do this; I think he regrets retiring so early,' replied Frances.

Margaret returned home, relieved at last to have put her finances in the hands of a capable, trusted friend. With a load off her mind, she was able to concentrate on her new home and her new friends from the Bible Study group. As she was newly widowed and noticeably impractical, the group had been especially supportive to her, and she was aware of this.

Apart from the recurring thoughts of the birth of baby Grace that still agitated her, she was living more at ease day to day.

Harold took some time to go over Margaret's finances, and when he had finished he came to her house and explained that he had simplified matters for her, and how she could now manage without difficulty. Margaret, pathetically grateful, could not do enough to let him know how much she appreciated the work he had done. He got up to go and put the papers down on the coffee table with the words: 'And my account is on the top of the pile, if you could please see to this shortly.' He shook hands with her and left.

Margaret looked at the account – it was for thousands of pounds. She reeled, as she had felt certain that Harold was doing this for her as a friend and not for a moment had she thought he would charge her; the bill was enormous and would reduce her capital a great deal. Feeling stunned by this turn of events, her body seized up and she did not know who to confide in.

'Of course, Patricia will understand. I will tell her and warn her to tell only Malcolm, no one else.' She phoned her immediately.

'I had got into a bit of a mess with my finances,' she said. 'Frances said her husband, who is a retired accountant, would sort it all out for me. As Frances is such a good friend and I've known her for many years, I was absolutely certain that Harold, her husband, would not charge me. I remember Ben helping Frances's brother out when he needed advice about stocks and shares; Ben helped a lot of people out in his lifetime, and he never charged one of them. I cannot believe Harold is charging me, and his bill is for thousands.'

This was a bit of a bombshell for Patricia. Remembering how lavishly they had lived with Ben, it had never occurred to her that her mother would ever lack money.

'Goodness, that really is a bit of a blow for you. Will it really make a big difference to your income?'

'Harold has told me the approximate income I will get each year,' replied Margaret. 'It's not what I have been having but I will still be reasonably well off.'

'That's all that matters, Mum. You don't want to be worrying about money at your age. You will get a monthly statement from your bank; if it shows you are spending more money than is coming into your account you will need to ease up a bit.'

Margaret, relieved to hear Patricia talk to her so calmly, felt better. She paid Harold's account, tried to be more careful with her money and found she had no trouble coping with her finances. But the whole issue of having been charged so many thousands of pounds by Harold had left a bad taste in her mouth and whenever anything the least bit stressful happened, her mind would jerk back to Gordon and baby Grace, and she would become agitated.

Chapter 22

Health Deterioration

The anxiety that Margaret had felt about her financial problems had taken its toll on her. Apart from the interest in her grandson, Kevin, Margaret felt herself degenerating. She was now seventy-four and starting to get forgetful of little things such as hairdressing or dental appointments. She even forgot the occasional women's group meeting, or the time of the Sunday morning service at church. She tried hard to cover these things up, saying something had prevented her from keeping the appointment, or the phone had rung, which had made her late, but as these instances became more frequent Margaret worried more and more. Mrs Glazebrook told her to keep a diary and write down the time of every meeting and of any appointment she made. But it had gone too far and Margaret panicked, knowing that she was losing her grip.

By this time, in 1976, Malcolm, Patricia and Kevin had moved to Birmingham, as Malcolm had been promoted, necessitating a move, but this was a two-hour drive from Margaret. When Patricia had told Margaret that they were going to move, it was a shock to her, as she had thought she would have her daughter near her for ever. She had said in a sorrowful voice: 'We've never been parted, this is the first time.'

But Patricia, busy planning the move and excited about Malcolm's new job, did not have the same emotions and replied: 'I know, but we will keep in touch a lot.'

Once in Birmingham, Patricia's hands were full settling into the new city and finding a school for Kevin. When she phoned her mother, Margaret gave no inkling that anything was wrong, and Patricia did not worry. But a few weeks after their move, Patricia had a phone call from one of the neighbours in the cul-de-sac where Margaret lived, who told her that Margaret had been coming to the front door in her underclothes and waving her arms about. Patricia was horrified and dropped everything to go to her mother, but when she got there, Margaret insisted that nothing was wrong and there was no problem. However, Patricia believed the lady who had phoned her and thought she should speak to Margaret's doctor.

'My mother's neighbour tells me she has been coming to the door in her underclothes and waving her arms about,' she told him. 'I'm concerned, as she lives alone and she is still driving.'

'Yes, she is a patient of mine, but she never comes to see me,' the doctor replied. 'I'll visit her this week and let you know what needs to be done. I'll also speak to the neighbour who has been in touch with you.'

The doctor kept his word and phoned Patricia in Birmingham to say: 'I have seen your mother and spoken to her neighbour, who mentioned that she had seen her on several occasions getting into her car and driving recklessly up the cul-de-sac far too fast. I have suggested an appointment with a psychiatrist.'

'Oh goodness,' gasped Patricia. 'I had not realised it was as bad as that.'

'I'm afraid it is,' he said, 'and I have made the appointment with Mr Sims for next week at Bromley hospital. Your mother's neighbour has kindly offered to take her to make sure she goes.'

Patricia responded: 'Once we know what should be done I will come up of course.'

'Good, then I'll know she'll have your support.'

Patricia told Malcolm what the doctor had said and they both recognised that Margaret's future was uncertain and that she would be looking to them for help and emotional support. Malcolm was one of four children and therefore any care or assistance his parents needed in the future would be shared between the four of them, but Patricia was the only child and Margaret had always leant on her, and particularly on Malcolm, when making decisions.

The psychiatrist's report recommended that Margaret have a stay in a psychiatric unit in Bromley hospital, so that they could see how she progressed, and whether she could return to her home or would need to go into a nursing or care home. Patricia went up to get Margaret settled into the psychiatric unit, but by then Margaret was muddled in her speech, she was seeing people across the room who were not there and describing events that had never happened. Patricia was shocked to find the change in her since her last visit, and she found it upsetting to see her mother like this, as she herself felt unsure quite how to cope. Returning home, she said to Malcolm: 'You can't imagine the change in her since the last time I saw her; she is not like my mother any more. What's more, I can't communicate with her – we cannot have any form of conversation. She kept saying that she was seeing Dorothy across the room which, of course, is rubbish. I suggested to her that we went across and spoke to Dorothy, so that Mother could see she was not there, but at that point she refused point blank to do this.'

'Goodness knows what will happen now,' replied Malcolm. 'We will have to be prepared to go up to see her at a moment's notice.'

Malcolm had always been a very good son-in-law to Margaret and he knew she depended on his advice. He had known from the start that she was not like his own mother, who was much more sensible and down-to-earth. Now this had happened he was prepared to do what he could for her.

Returning to stay the weekend at her mother's house in Chislehurst two weeks later, Patricia found her mother no better and still under the care of a psychiatrist in Bromley hospital. The psychiatrist spoke with Patricia and advised that her mother would need a care home or nursing home that accepted people with disturbed minds. Patricia, still distressed to see Margaret like this, set about finding a home that was agreeable to taking Margaret. She thought it would be easy to find a pleasant, comfortable home but it was not. After phoning four nursing homes, none of whom would consider taking someone whose mind was disturbed, she finally found one in Shortlands, not far from the hospital, who asked her to come in to discuss it. The home seemed clean and the staff efficient yet pleasant with the patients. It was not luxurious, but Matron seemed kind and understood that Patricia was living in Birmingham and therefore would not be able to be around most of the time, but if Margaret's physical health deteriorated they would keep her. Although not one hundred per cent happy to move Margaret into a nursing home of any kind, Patricia felt this was the best she could do for her mother. It was agreed that Margaret would move there the following week.

Before going home, Patricia explained all this to Margaret, who seemed to take it in without getting upset, but said she would prefer to stay in the hospital, and so Patricia left her without pressing her to agree to move to the nursing home. She got home in time to be there when twelve-year-old Kevin got back from school and was glad to return to normality. She told him: 'I think I will have to go back to Granny's house next weekend. I can't let her be moved to the nursing home without me there.'

'Is Granny ill,' Kevin asked.

'She is old now, and when you get old your brain sometimes gets tired and you get very muddled and cannot look after yourself. That is why she has to have people to look after her,' Patricia replied.

'Is she going to die,' Kevin asked.

'At some point we are all going to die, and as Granny is much older than any of us it is likely she will die before us.'

'Oh, I see. Will I know when she dies?'

Patricia sighed. 'Yes, I'll tell you. I promise you I'll do that.'

Kevin seemed satisfied with this answer, and they did not talk about it again that day.

Patricia found that she was anxious about her mother and it was on her mind hourly. In the middle of the week, as she was tidying Kevin's bedroom, the phone rang. It was one of the psychiatric nurses from Bromley hospital: 'I am sorry to tell you, but your mother was walking across the ward when she had a fall. An X-ray shows she has broken her femur. The surgeon has reset it and she is now coming round from the anaesthetic.'

'Oh dear, this certainly is a blow,' replied Patricia. 'How is she?'

'It remains to be seen; a broken femur is serious in someone of her age. I would leave it a couple of days before coming to see her.'

'Yes, I will,' said Patricia. 'Thank you, I'll be there at the end of the week.'

'We will, of course, let you know if there is any change.'

After hearing this news Patricia felt shaky. Margaret had always been in control of herself and she could not imagine her lying in bed inactive.

When Malcolm came home she told him about the phone call. 'It's bad enough that my mother has a disturbed mind and needs psychiatric care, but to have broken her femur, that's even worse.'

'Go up at the weekend,' said Malcolm. 'I can look after Kevin, it will not be a problem.'

'Yes, I will, thank you; it seems one thing after another.'

Travelling up on the train on the following Friday, Patricia had time to reflect on the situation. She thought: 'I suppose that when we get old we can't cope with things in the way we used to. All the same, I hate seeing my mother like this. And she must hate it too. The psychiatrist told me to always bring her back into reality, but it seems a losing battle.'

At the hospital, Patricia walked through the corridors to reach Margaret's ward.

'It is so depressing being in a hospital,' she sighed to herself. 'Miles and miles of endless walkways to find the right ward. How people work here I do not know.'

However, Margaret was sitting in a chair when she arrived, and greeted her normally.

'Darling, how good of you to come and see me. Nurse told me you were coming, and I have been looking forward to seeing you.'

Patricia was astonished to hear her mother speak like this, she seemed so much better in her mind. She was about to reply when a nurse came up and asked if she could speak to her alone.

'It is such good news. Your mother has recovered her memory and appears to be completely in her right mind. It could have been the operation or the anaesthetic that has jolted her back to her normal self.'

'What a relief; thank you so much for telling me.'

'But she will be frail after breaking her femur and will require nursing for a long time. We are moving her to an orthopaedic ward until she is able to go to a care home,' said the nurse.

'Of course, I understand.'

Patricia went back to Margaret and the two of them were able to carry on an ordinary conversation, which Patricia found amazing. Margaret asked about Malcolm and Kevin – which she had not done for months. Patricia's state of anxiety for the past few months lessened and her mood lifted at once. She realised her mother was now fragile and needed care for the rest of her life, but she had got her mind back and could communicate with people normally.

'What a difference this will make to her,' she thought, 'and to everyone else around her.'

She went home and spent some time on the phone to her church friends, especially the women's groups Margaret belonged to. Her neighbours in the cul-de-sac were relieved to hear the news, as they had wondered if she would be coming home. Margaret was, in fact, held in great esteem by the community – many people could remember her during the years she had lived at Greenacres with Ben and her generosity towards charities and to those who had fallen on hard times was not forgotten.

The women's groups were formed of strong Christian women who were not prepared to ignore Margaret now that she was frail and in hospital and all were anxious to keep in touch with her once she was settled in a care home. Patricia again spoke on the phone to the nursing home in Shortlands and Matron confirmed they would still take Margaret.

Once again Patricia did the trip to Chislehurst to see her mother, and when she spoke to Margaret about the home, this time Margaret seemed perfectly agreeable to going there. She had recovered amazingly well from the broken femur and was able to walk well with a stick.

'I'd like to take you there tomorrow while I am still in Chislehurst,' Patricia said. 'You will be able to meet Matron, see your room and look around the place.'

'I'd like that,' said Margaret. 'I know I am not able to look after myself now, I feel too weak, and the least little effort tires me out. As well as that, I have got used to my meals being brought to me, and if I am tired nurse helps me to wash.'

Patricia felt her eyes filling with tears on hearing this, as although Margaret had more or less recovered her mind, she had lost a lot of weight and it was obvious that she was very thin and fragile. Seeing her like this Patricia felt an immense sense of loss for the strong mother she had always been. Margaret and Patricia had always been tied together with an unbreakable bond, and at this time Patricia knew nothing of Margaret's pregnancy and baby Grace.

A nurse was passing and Patricia caught up with her. 'It feels so odd to see my mother like this; she has always been a pillar of strength for me.'

'Well, she will need to draw on *your* strength now. Just be there for her when you can,' replied the nurse.

'I will. In fact, it is possible that my husband's job is moving back to London, so we will be living in this area, which will be a good thing.'

Patricia went back to say goodbye to Margaret, who caught her hand and said: 'There is something I want to tell you, darling; something that happened when I was young. I have never told you before, but I want to tell you now.'

Unfortunately, by then visiting hours were over and Patricia had to leave. However, she was staying another day and she promised Margaret that she would be back to see her then. As she left, Margaret looked at her intently with a regretful gaze and Patricia could see how distressed she was.

'What on earth could my mother want to tell me,' Patricia thought. She spoke to Malcolm that night on the phone and neither of them could think of anything.

'Anyway, I'll know tomorrow morning,' she said. 'And I'll be glad to catch the afternoon train home.'

That night Patricia thought uneasily about what Margaret had said, and especially the look that had crossed her face as Patricia left.

Chapter 23

Confession

The following morning on the dot of ten-thirty, Patricia hastened up to the orthopaedic ward to collect Margaret. The ward was looking neat and tidy and coffee had just been brought round but Margaret was not drinking hers.

'Mummy, your coffee is getting cold; try and have it while it's still hot'.

Margaret made no attempt to drink the coffee and replied: 'I have something I want to tell you.'

'That's fine, go right ahead, I'm listening.'

Margaret began. 'You remember I grew up in Darjeeling, where I was the only girl with seven brothers. We lived in a quiet residential neighbourhood and were a happy family, not wealthy, but the British in India lived well in those days. My father was well known, as he was the Traffic Inspector for the city, or Stationmaster as it was called. It was considered a responsible job since, at that time, trains were unreliable, and passengers depended on him for the latest information. Our family – we were Catholics – were regarded with respect. When I was twenty-four my comfortable life suddenly changed. I remember the afternoon so well. It was the autumn of 1926, and I had returned from a visit to the city. I was in absolute turmoil, as I had just discovered that I was pregnant.'

'Were you married then?' asked Patricia.

'No, I was not married, that was the problem. I had fallen deeply in love with a Scotsman called Gordon. We started an affair, though I had never looked on it like that, as I was sure he was going to marry me. Two and a half months later I suspected I might be pregnant and when I went to our British doctor he confirmed that I was. I immediately told Gordon, but he was not at all pleased and told me that he was already married and intended to stay that way.'

Patricia sat still, silent and dismayed. Her mother, pregnant by a married man? She could not imagine her rather conventional and often tight-lipped mother had kept a secret like this throughout her life. In her shock and confusion, she wondered if she could have been the baby.

'Mummy, was it me?' she asked.

'No, it wasn't you. In those days a white woman in India becoming pregnant when she was not married was totally unacceptable. I could not tell my parents, nor any of my brothers.'

'How simply awful for you. How things have changed now. What did you do?'

'That evening my eldest brother, Howard, who lived in Bombay, was home for a family visit. In absolute desperation I told him everything, and, of course, he was terribly shocked. However, he said he would take me with him when he returned to Bombay and I could stay until the baby was born and he would pass me off as a young widow. He would tell our parents it would give me a chance to live in a different city, and I might even find a good husband there. I cried with relief, as suddenly there seemed a way out of my predicament. So, I went to Bombay with Howard for the pregnancy, and Howard made me comfortable in his apartment.'

Margaret's face was troubled as she recalled all this, and she was clasping her top sheet with both hands.

'So, you were in an unknown city while you were pregnant?' ventured Patricia.

'Yes, but my brother had saved me from total disgrace by taking me to Bombay. He found me a wonderful British doctor who looked after me and became a good friend and delivered my baby.'

'Was it a boy or a girl?'

'It was a beautiful baby girl. I called her Grace and was with her for four days in the hospital. I desperately wanted to keep her, but I had no money and as white women did not work in those days I had no choice but to give her up, to a well-to-do British family living in Jubbulpore. I can remember now how I felt the day I gave her to them, I felt something was being torn out of me.'

Patricia was silent for a while, reliving what Margaret had told her.

Margaret continued: 'We told everyone that the baby had been stillborn. When I left the hospital without Grace I felt sick and dizzy and could hardly walk down the corridor. From that moment I have thought about her every day of my life, I have wondered where she is, how she is and what her life is like now. I went back to Howard's apartment and after a while he urged me to be more social and to find a husband; it was the last thing I wanted to do.'

'I can imagine how appalling you felt, giving up your baby,' said Patricia. 'Oh, what a sad story, Mummy. I had no idea you had been through anything like this. Why haven't you told me before?'

'I have tried to hide it from you and everyone else to give you a better life. I wanted you to have a life unlike mine, and so you have. As soon as I recovered from the birth I did as Howard suggested, I went to every social event possible and met a number of men. In time I met Edwyn, your father, and we became engaged. This proved to be a real blessing, as Edwyn was living in England and it meant I could leave India behind, forget everything and start a new life there. But I was wrong, as I have never forgotten Grace; I remember her every single day, and sometimes it has even stopped me enjoying having you. And worst of all I know that God can never forgive me – I will die unforgiven.'

'Goodness, Mummy, how can you possibly feel that? Surely you know that the Bible is all about forgiveness. Can't you believe this?'

'Not for me, God cannot forgive me.'

This was said in such a convincing way that it had a most uneasy effect on Patricia; she started to reason with her mother, but she could see that she was set in her belief. She changed the subject to turn Margaret's mind in a different direction.

'I know Jennifer and Fiona from your women's group have been to see you. They have told me they would like to see you again. Shall I arrange a time for this?'

'I'd like to see them to tell them what I have told you; I feel close to them and I think they will understand,' replied Margaret.

'I'll phone them both today, Mummy; I'm sure they'll come in tomorrow. We can go to the nursing home the day after.'

Patricia left in a daze, stunned by what Margaret had told her and appalled that her mother had had to live her life keeping this guilty secret. She herself had been taken aback to hear she had a half-sister somewhere, possibly in India. How extraordinary! It explained a lot to Patricia, especially why she had often seen her mother with pursed lips for no apparent reason; it must have been when conversations or events had touched her about her past.

Jennifer and Fiona came the following morning, and Margaret told her story all over again. They were both strongly affected to hear it, especially Margaret's insistence that God could never forgive her. They urged and urged her to accept God's forgiveness, but it was of no use. They went away and came back in the afternoon with the suggestion that they would hold a healing service for her. With much reluctance Margaret agreed to this, but as she was moving to the nursing home that week they decided to let her settle down before holding the service.

Moving to the nursing home was a big step for Margaret; the routine there was quite different from that in the hospital and she had to get used to the way it was run. However, she seemed pleased to have her own room, and Patricia had seen that a few pieces of her treasured furniture were taken there. There was a very pleasant day room in which the newspapers and magazines were put, but she could not be persuaded to go in there. Although she was now in her right mind, the one thing she dwelt on was that God would not be able to forgive her. After a few attempts Patricia felt it was useless to attempt to change her mind and she did not try.

Two weeks later Jennifer and Fiona arranged a small healing service in Jennifer's home and several other members of the women's group said they would also like to be there. Patricia did not go, as she found it too painful to see Margaret so distressed by thinking that God could not forgive her; the people in the women's group were her mother's age and, Patricia felt, very much more suited than her to hold the service.

On the day of the service they collected Margaret early to give her time to settle down – she was wearing a dowdy dress, most unlike her usual fashionable outfits. She knew Jennifer's home well, so it did not feel strange to her. Members came in quietly and focussed their attention on

Margaret. When the service started, they sang part of the hymn, 'Abide with Me', then Jennifer spoke, reminding the group that God tells us that He is always there to forgive our sins, whatever they are. Fiona reminded the group of the story in the Bible of the woman taken in adultery. The Pharisees urged Jesus to say she should be stoned, but Jesus said that no one is without sin, and He did not condemn her and she is 'to go and sin no more'. Jennifer and Fiona both laid hands on Margaret, and Jennifer said a short prayer, bringing her before God for forgiveness of a sin committed long ago and ending the prayer with thanks that Margaret had been forgiven. As the service ended, everyone took Communion, but Margaret pushed the bread and wine away – she did not say anything, but she physically refused to take it.

When the service had finished those present were naturally distressed at Margaret's refusal to take Communion and to not accept God's forgiveness; they tried once again to persuade her, but it was of no use. She remained adamant in her attitude and indeed was forceful in insisting on it. Nothing would change her view, so Jennifer and Fiona took her back to the nursing home, and Jennifer said: 'Margaret, my dear, you have been one of the most committed and generous members of our group for some time now and we have all come to love you. We know that you are feeling desperately unhappy and we are not going to leave you feeling like this: we are going to continue to pray that you will be healed and able to take Communion and finally accept God's forgiveness.'

'God cannot forgive me, Jennifer. I know this,' replied Margaret.

'Yes, Margaret, He can, and the Bible says He forgives all sinners. Try and repeat to yourself throughout each day that God forgives all sinners.'

Margaret did not reply, so Jennifer and Fiona left her. They let Matron know what had taken place that afternoon, and she was not unsympathetic to their actions.

Patricia continued to visit Margaret three afternoons a week. She found her mother to be low and depressed, and Patricia could not find any matter of interest that caught her attention. She and Malcolm were now living in Margaret's house in Chislehurst, as his job had temporarily moved to London. Since Margaret was now in the nursing home, it seemed the right thing to do, as it allowed Patricia to be reasonably nearby to visit her. She noticed that her mother felt worthless and was only prepared to wear clothes from charity shops. All her life she had worn stylish and elegant clothes, but now they hung in her wardrobe at home unused.

Seeing her mother like this had a disheartening effect on Patricia. She would say to her friends: 'I don't feel I am reaching her, as she's not able to respond to facts or logic. If I quote the Bible to her she just says something like "Not for me". I feel I'm no use to her, but then neither is anyone else. The staff at the nursing home are so good, they accept her as she is. I'm particularly worried at the moment, as Malcolm's new job is in Swindon, and this means we will have to move to that area, and it will be more difficult for me to see my mother as often as I do.'

Patricia was herself low since, as an only child, she had carried the burden of Margaret's breakdown alone for two years, and with the move in view she was feeling rather bleak. Malcolm was marvellous; he had always been a support to Margaret and in the past she had frequently turned to him for advice. He could see now how anxious Patricia was and how stressful it was for her to see her mother in this state.

Chapter 24

The Closing Stages

In 1978 Margaret had been in the nursing home in Shortlands for two years. Now that they were living in Cirencester, for Malcolm's job in Swindon, it was not so easy for Patricia to go and see Margaret. It meant driving to Kemble station then taking two train journeys and a taxi to the nursing home. When she did this, Patricia usually stayed two nights at Margaret's house so that she could see her twice. Although Patricia had Power of Attorney for Margaret, she decided not to sell her house since it was so convenient for her when she was able to come and see her mother.

The weeks passed and Patricia went regularly to see Margaret, returning home dejected and depleted of energy. Then one morning in 1980 the phone rang in Cirencester. It was a nurse from the nursing home to say that Margaret had had a small heart attack and had been taken into Bromley hospital. It had only been a week since Patricia had been to see her, but she packed a small case and caught the first train possible.

Arriving at Bromley hospital she walked as quickly as she could through the endless corridors to find the right ward. Margaret was lying in bed, awake, and she knew it was Patricia immediately.

'Mummy, how are you? I came as soon as I heard about your heart attack.'

Margaret was slow to respond, but in time she said very slowly: 'I'm all right, darling. I feel all right, in fact very all right.'

'You are not all right, Mummy, you've had a heart attack.'

Margaret could only speak very deliberately and seemed to choose her words carefully.

'I know, but in fact I feel better than I have done for ages. I am not in pain, but I do feel very, very weak.'

'Oh Mummy, you are not well, but you do look much better in yourself than you have done for a long time.'

'I don't know why, but things seem clearer now and I'm feeling calm.'

'Oh, I am so, so glad,' said Patricia, with relief.

Margaret continued slowly: 'I made a big mistake when I was young, and I have stupidly spent my life believing in a God who could not forgive me. I do not know now if there is a God or not: if there is, He will forgive me and if there is not a God it does not matter. I now feel perfectly calm.'

A weight rolled off Patricia's shoulders; what she had dreaded was that Margaret would die in misery, feeling God could not forgive her. 'I am so, so happy, Mummy, to hear that; it is all I have hoped for you and now you must get better.'

'Maybe, but all I want is to keep feeling as I do now, so content and comfortable, it is wonderful to be like this.' Margaret's voice was slow; she was exhausted.

'You must just rest now, I'll go but I'm staying at your house and will come in again tomorrow morning,' said Patricia.

Margaret looked very drained but totally tranquil. Patricia kissed her and the nurse told her they would phone if there was any change. She got home and phoned Malcolm, and he said he would come up on the evening train, which he did.

The following morning the hospital rang at seven in the morning to say they should come at once, as Margaret would probably not last long. Malcolm and Patricia went as quickly as they could, and when they arrived Margaret was propped up on her pillows, her eyes shut. Patricia said: 'Malcolm and I are here; we have come to be with you.'

Margaret spoke to them, saying quite clearly: 'Are you waiting for me?'

They both smiled. This was something she would often say when she stayed with them and they were going out somewhere.

Patricia said: 'Yes, Mummy, we are all ready to go with you now.'

Margaret opened her eyes and smiled, she looked totally composed. Two minutes later they could see she was slipping away. Patricia kissed her mother and their eyes met for the last time. Margaret closed her eyes and five minutes later she was gone – all the remorse of the past years had been resolved in time for her to go in peace. She was seventy-seven and had remained a beautiful woman until the day she died.

All rights reserved

About the Author

Patricia Young was educated at a public school in England. After a spell in Paris to learn French, she studied Clinical Theology, which focused her awareness on personality differences. Her previous book, *Understanding your Personality*, was translated into seven languages.

Patricia had always wondered about her mother's life – noticing that she was often edgy and it seemed she was holding things back. It was not until near her death that her mother broke down and Patricia was finally told of the event that had blighted her mother's life and haunted her daily. Since then Patricia has pieced together that extraordinary life and now, in *The Raj, the Rolls and the Remorse*, she uses her knowledge of personality to write the story of what her mother went through.

Printed in Great Britain
by Amazon